MEDIEVAL MARRIAGE

The Johns Hopkins Symposia in Comparative History

The Johns Hopkins Symposia in Comparative History arc occasional volumes sponsored by the Department of History at The Johns Hopkins University and The Johns Hopkins University Press, comprising original essays by leading scholars in the United States and other countries. Each volume considers, from a comparative perspective, an important topic of current historical interest. The present volume is the eleventh. Its preparation has been assisted by the Phillip W. Haberman, Jr., Foundation.

MEDIEVAL MARRIAGE
Two Models from Twelfth-Century France

by GEORGES DUBY

Translated by ELBORG FORSTER

THE JOHNS HOPKINS UNIVERSITY PRESS
Baltimore and London

The Johns Hopkins Symposia in Comparative History, Number 11

Originally published in hardcover, 1978
Johns Hopkins Paperbacks edition, 1991

The Johns Hopkins University Press, 701 West 40th Street,
Baltimore, Maryland 21211-2190
The Johns Hopkins Press Ltd., London

The paper used in this publication meets the minimum requirements of
American National Standard for Information Sciences—Permanence of Paper
for Printed Library Materials, ANSI Z39.48-1984.

Library of Congress Catalog Card Number 77-17255
ISBN 0-8018-4319-7

Library of Congress Cataloging in Publication data will be found on the last
printed page of this book.

Contents

Foreword

When Sidney Painter, the distinguished professor of medieval history at Johns Hopkins, used to talk about his plans after retirement, he often said, with the pleasure of anticipation, that he would devote himself to a history of marriage in the Middle Ages. Unfortunately, his sudden and untimely death in 1960, at the height of his scholarly momentum, robbed us of this as well as his other projects. Nonetheless, as early as the 1950s Sidney Painter had the imagination to identify an important historical problem. While he had not yet found time to approach the history of marriage directly, he left some suggestions as to how he would have proceeded. A genealogist by talent (he was incapable of forgetting the most distant cousin of a baronial family tree), he was never content with genealogy as an end, but used it to pursue the larger goals of social history. His last article, "The Family and the Feudal System in Twelfth-Century England,"[1] which appeared posthumously, applied this minute knowledge of family histories to the larger social developments of the English medieval baronage. And in the process he implicitly recognized the importance of a social perspective on medieval marriage that had not yet found its historian.

When the Department of History at Johns Hopkins invited Georges Duby to deliver the James S. Schouler Lectures for 1977, it received with more than usual pleasure not only his acceptance but also his proposal to treat the history of medieval marriage. Since his election to the Collège de France in 1970, Georges Duby has drawn to his weekly seminar at the Collège most of the leading medievalists of Paris, even of France, trained in the greatly diverse disciplines applicable to the Middle Ages. Faithful to his promise when his new chair of "medieval societies" was established at the Collège, he has enlisted their collaboration and inspired their efforts toward the broad themes of social history. Since this seminar has been discussing the subjects of family, kinship, marriage, and sexuality in the Middle Ages for a number of years, the present work presents the first fruits of this particular collaborative enterprise.

As in his brilliant book *Le dimanche de Bouvines*,[2] Georges Duby adopts the approach of exemplarism in this present study. Whereas the former developed the sociology of medieval warfare from the specific battle of Bouvines in 1214, the latter raises two examples from twelfth-century France to investigate medieval marriage. After a preliminary chapter in which he sketches the outlines of the aristocratic and ecclesiastical views toward matrimony, Georges Duby probes in rich detail the marriages and divorces of the kings of France in the twelfth century. Lest the reader object that royalty, by the height of its social position and authority, was unrepresentative of aristocratic society, he devotes a final chapter to the Flemish counts of Guines based on a reading of the chronicle of Lambert d'Ardres. The texts on which he bases his research and the events which he recounts will not be new to medieval historians, who, for the most part, have used them for political narrative and the development of monarchical and seigneurial institutions. Georges Duby, however, employs them for the first time to depict two radically different views of marriage, the ecclesiastical and the aristocratic, which conflicted and finally accommodated with each other during the twelfth century.

In his inaugural address at the Collège de France, Georges Duby dedicated himself to the study of medieval societies in their globality, that included their mental perceptions as well. This present book on medieval marriage is another fulfillment of that promise. Like Philippe Ariès's preceding lectures at Johns Hopkins on attitudes towards death,[3] it is an essay intended to open up a new terrain of social history. Not a definitive summation, but an exploratory probe, it hopes to entice others to follow its lead.

The three chapters contained in this volume were originally presented in French as lectures at the Johns Hopkins University on 12, 13, and 15 April 1977. The audience was furnished with English translations prepared beforehand by Elborg Forster; these translations, with slight revisions and the addition of footnotes, are published in the present book. On behalf of the author and the Department of History I would like to thank her for her care in seeing the translation through the press.

JOHN W. BALDWIN

Baltimore
August 1977

MEDIEVAL MARRIAGE

I.

Two Models of Marriage:
The Aristocratic
and the Ecclesiastical

The historian of marriage in the medieval West faces a vast field from which the thickets have been cleared only in spots. Those who want to do useful work here must begin by delineating the confines of the area where they will carry out their research. With all due prudence, I intend to do this in the following manner: Since I am neither a canonist, a liturgist, nor a theologian, I have chosen to consider marriage from the perspective of social history and, more precisely, to observe the practices of marriage.[1] In choosing this course, I have not exactly made things easy for myself. For most of the texts that have come down to us reveal not the practice, but the theory of marriage. These

The translator gratefully acknowledges the help of John W. Baldwin, who closely followed the preparation of this translation.

documents tell us what was considered normal. They can be used as sources for the reconstruction of a system of values, a body of moral rules, a code that demarcates the limits between licit and illicit behavior. This image of an ideal order quite obviously did shape individual behavior, but only imperfectly. I should like to break through this incrustation of prescriptions, which has hitherto absorbed the attention of almost all scholars in the field, in order to come as close as possible to the living realities. This difficult undertaking has been pursued for several years now in my seminar at the Collège de France. I am well aware that this work is only just beginning and that the findings I shall present here are very incomplete and mainly designed to emphasize certain points.

At this stage I must limit my investigation to the one, very thin, layer of lay society which is beginning to emerge from obscurity, and by that I mean the high aristocracy. Moreover, I am concentrating on only one part of Europe, where the documentary material is a little richer than elsewhere, that is, the north of the kingdom of France, and on one century, the twelfth. I have chosen this period not simply because it is particularly familiar to me, but for two more compelling reasons. For, on the one hand, after the great drought of the tenth and the early eleventh centuries, the sources become more abundant. In particular, one can now examine literary works written for the entertainment of knights and princes, works which may not reflect what they did, but at least what they wanted to do. On the other hand, it seems to me that a major shift in the evolution of the institution of marriage occurred in our culture at that time. For this was the beginning of a decisive phase in the conflict that dominated this entire evolution, the conflict between two radically different and antagonistic models—the lay model of marriage, created to safeguard the social order, and the ecclesiastical model, created to safeguard the divine order. Of these two models, only the second is clearly visible, since our information comes almost exclusively from churchmen. But then these men were constantly fighting the first model, denouncing, condemning, and consequently describing it. Sound method demands, I believe, that I begin by presenting a cursory outline of these two opposing systems.

Contrary to what is sometimes said even now, society, that is, the high society of the twelfth century, appears to have rested for a long time on a fundamental unit, the household or two-generation family. This was the triangle formed by the father, mother, and children, around which were clustered other individuals in varying number, some unmarried relatives, all those "provided for" by the household, and the *familia*, the team of domestic servants. The framework within which this group became aware of its cohesion was the house or *domus*. Because the specific function of those who spoke of their noble status traditionally was and remained military, males occupied a dominant position in all noble houses, although the wife of the head of the household, the "lady," was also entrusted with important functions, being in charge of the household economy, the female servants, and the young children.[2] This basic structure shaped an entire set of attitudes, especially those of respect and deference.[3] So compelling was this structure that every metaphor that sought to express power relationships—whether between feudal lord and vassal, within the seigneury, the principality, or the kingdom—in some way made use of the image of the house. And it was this structure that placed marriage at the core of all social institutions.

By uniting two individuals born of two different houses in order to found a new house of similar form— or, rather, to ensure the survival of one of these houses—marriage bestowed official recognition and singled out among all possible unions those that society legitimized as a means of perpetuating itself without endangering its structural stability. This is why marriage was not supposed to be clandestine, but rather an ostensible, ceremonial act. It called for celebration, a very public celebration, which, for a time, assembled large numbers of people attending a central rite, namely, the procession that conveyed a woman, the bride, to a house, a chamber, a bed, in the expectation that she would soon become a mother. Marriage thus inserted procreation into an order of things. And order also implied peace, because the institution of marriage was the very opposite of abduction. It was founded on an agreement, a treaty, known as the marriage pact (*pactum conjugale*), that was concluded between two houses. Under such a pact, one of the houses would give up, the other receive or acquire, a woman. The exchange, then, involved a woman, or, more precisely, her anticipated motherhood, her "blood" and all that it brought to the new family in terms of both ancestral force (*virtus*) and claims to inheritances. Certain rites expressing this contract were therefore associated with the ceremony. These were three gestures that are known to us because they became part of the ecclesiastical ritual used in the period and the region under study here:[4] the giving away of the bride in the rite of divesting and investing by the placing of hands, the countergift to the dowry, the *dos*, given by the bridegroom in the form of a ring or a few coins as a token of his granting a claim to the property of the new household, and finally the kneeling of the bride before the man who became her "master," a gesture designed to affirm that she was handed over to the power of another male, no longer the head of the house from which she came, but of the house she was entering. The ceremony of agreement, the betrothal (*desponsatio*), naturally preceded that of transfer, the marriage (*nuptiae*). Sometimes these two solemn occasions were separated by a long interval, since it was often expedient to conclude the alliance long before the practical circumstances, especially the age of the parties, made their physical union possible.

At this point, three observations should be made:

1. The marriage pact was essential to the future of both houses. Thus, the decision was too important to be left to the individuals concerned and was therefore made by those who had the responsibility for the two families.

2. The agreement had different consequences for the two families. One of them introduced a foreign body into its midst, namely, the bride who became part

of the household. To some extent, this woman always remained an intruder, the object of tenacious distrust, of a suspicion that was was invariably focused upon her should some unusual misfortune befall her husband. The other family, however, had sacrificed some of its substance and sought compensation, and that is why we often see particularly close ties of affection (*dilectio*) between the children of the new couple and their mother's brothers.

3. The terms of the contract, finally, guaranteed the married woman autonomous rights, both to her dower (*dos*) and to her expectations of inheritance. However, there is no doubt that in practice these rights were exercised by men, namely, by her husband, by her brothers if she became widowed, and by her sons and heirs, in whose hands, during the next generation, the paternal and maternal inheritances became one.[5] It is a fact that in this society women never emerged from the strictest subordination. As Bishop Gilbert of Limerick put it so well, they submitted to their husbands whom they "served."[6]

This lay society had long ago worked out a system of rules concerning marriage, the organization of which can be dimly perceived. This system was designed, first and foremost, to protect all those who were not securely lodged within a conjugal situation. Widows and orphans were commended to the special care first of kings, then of princes, and soon of all knights as the "poor" par excellence. So were "ladies" and "maidens" whenever they left the protective enclosure of the house;[7] and even unmarried males, whose right to companionship (*contubernium*) was guaranteed and who found shelter within the complementary kin group that was formed by the company of vassals. This system, moreover, was also designed to protect the patrimony, to maintain the economic position of children born of wedded couples. This goal was at the root of the three salient features of the lay code of marriage.

1. Under this ethic, marriage, I repeat, regulated the sexual impulses, but only in the interest of a patrimony. As long as no inheritance was involved, sexual activity was permitted outside of marriage. On the other hand, it was of the utmost importance that a wife receive only one seed, that of her husband, lest intruders issued from another man's blood take their place among the claimants to the ancestral inheritance. This is why the moral code of the laity rigorously condemned adultery on the part of the woman.

2. This moral code did not require a monogamous structure. Widowers were perfectly free to remarry, and a husband could repudiate his wife. This was permissible not only, as one would expect, in case of adultery but also if it seemed to be in the interest of the patrimony to take another wife, either because the former wife was slow to give her husband the son who would carry on the house or, quite simply, because it seemed advantageous to the house to receive a woman of greater value. The important thing was that the repudiation take place in an orderly manner, by arrangement between the two families. It was at this point that the clauses of the *pactum* assumed their full signifi-

cance. Altogether, then, this moral code rigorously condemned violence and was particularly emphatic in its disapproval of abduction.[8]

3. Lastly, there was a strong tendency toward endogamy, for families frequently felt that a marriage between cousins could be used to reunite the scattered portions of inheritances disassembled in previous generations. Thus, while marriage remained forbidden within the house itself and within the close family group, the notion of incest came to lose all rigor beyond the third degree of kinship.

It appears that in this region the function of marriage within aristocratic society assumed ever greater importance as the social system we call feudalism took shape in the wake of the slow but irresistible structural mutation the dominant class had so recently experienced. Henceforth the values of chivalry—that is, the military vocation of this social category—were to be praised more resoundingly than ever, just as the benefits of individual adventure were to be celebrated in the myths of chivalric literature.[9] The fact is, however, that by then the economic preeminence of the aristocracy was no longer primarily dependent on the distribution of the spoils of war, as it had been in the eighth century, or on the legalized pillage of Church property, as it had been in the tenth and the first half of the eleventh centuries (for, among other things, the Church reform of the eleventh century had also put an end to the depredations of the laity). On the other hand, such preeminence was not yet primarily dependent, as it was to be after the thirteenth century, on pensions and wages or on the distribution of the revenues of princely finance. More than at any other time, the economic preeminence of the aristocracy depended on the resources of a patrimony and on the hereditary power to exploit the land and men.[10] More distinctly than either their forebears or their descendents, the knights of the twelfth century were basically inheritors. This process of taking root in an agrarian environment, as well as the gradual dissolution of private military companies, the granting of property to vassals, and the irrepressible evolution that changed feudal tenure to a hereditary right—all this served to ensconce the lay aristocracy more solidly than ever within the confines of the house (*domus*). It also explains why, ever since the second third of the eleventh century, the name of the house tended to become the common surname of all the offspring of the "race."[11] Under these circumstances it is appropriate to view chivalric society as an assembly of juxtaposed houses.

But I should say of a *certain number* of houses, for actually this number became fixed. Henceforth each root-stock sent forth only one stem. The adventitious branches were made to wither, so as not to sap the strength of the central trunk. Leaving, for a moment, the geographical limits I have set for myself and speaking from my knowledge of the Mâcon region, I have the very definite impression that in that area the widespread dissolution of the great Carolingian estates, which throughout the whole tenth century had led to a proliferation of noble houses, came to a halt during the second half of the eleventh and during the twelfth century.[12] And I also believe that one of the most effective causes of this emerging stability was the gradual spreading among all levels of aristocratic society of a lineage-oriented family structure that was modeled upon the royal example.[13] It had become clear that a tightening of the lineage structures was the most reliable means of safeguarding the patrimony, the very foundation of chivalric preeminence. (I might add, parenthetically, that at this time the rising productivity of the land made this patrimony more and more profitable, even though these ever-increasing resources were not always sufficient to cover the ever-rising expenditures demanded of those who would maintain their rank.)

Gradually adopting a monarchical cast, the house (*domus*) therefore strengthened the authority of the one man whom a certain Mâconnais charter calls the "head of the house" (*caput mansi*)[14] and whom Galbert of Bruges designated as the "head of the clan" (*caput generis*).[15] By virtue of an emerging principle of devolution based on the order of primogeniture, this authority fell to the eldest male. In order to curb the proliferation of potential heirs and to avoid divided inheritances, this head of the household, advised by his male relatives, came to pursue increasingly restrictive matrimonial strategies. Briefly stated, these amounted to a continuation of the policy of marrying off all the daughters of the house in order to create a widespread network of alliances—and this had always been, and still was, the policy of royal houses. But at the same time, every care had to be taken not to cut into the lineage's fortune. In other words, the house was willing to give up the blood of its women, but restricted their claims to the ancestral inheritance. And while every house was bent on ensuring its survival through the marriage of a son, it tried to marry only one, namely, the eldest. The house also saw to it that other sons did not take a legitimate wife, unless she was an heiress, for such a woman had no brother and was the eldest of a house that her husband would take over himself. The consequences of such a policy are evident. First of all, the supply of women was much greater than that of males in what one is tempted to call the marriage market. Those who had a son to marry could therefore seek out and obtain wives of better lineage and higher rank. This is why genealogical references so frequently extolled the preeminent "nobility" of the ancestors on the maternal side.[16] Secondly, most of the knights remained "youths," that is, bachelors.

I have elsewhere described this social phenomenon, so evident in twelfth-century northern France.[17] These were the turbulent bands of young men (*juvenes*), lateral members of a house where they had no authority, whether it was their own, where their father or older brother was in charge, or that of the patron where they had found shelter. I have also referred to the frustrations inherent in this position. Bound together though it was by its adherence to the chivalric ideal, this high stratum of lay society eventually experienced a deep fissure that was to become its principal line of cleavage. This was the distinction between those who were elders and those who were not yet—and in most cases would never be—*seniores*, between the married men (*conjugati*) and the "bachelors"; that is, between elder and younger sons. (I might add that the vocabulary used and the mental connotations underlying these words indicate that this fundamental disposition had its precise equivalent in the relationship of subordination within equality inherent in the vassalic obligation.) All power was in the hands of the elders (*seniores*), the eldest sons, married men, and heads of their own houses. They represented the principle of order in aristocratic society. Under these circumstances, marriage assumed extraordinary importance. It had always been a crucial stage in a woman's life, for at marriage a girl became a *domina*, the "lady" of a house, part of whose internal authority was placed into her hands. Henceforth, marriage came to be perceived as an event that transformed a man's life perhaps even more profoundly.[18] To a young man, marrying meant leaving behind his unsteady existence, his troubled and impetuous wanderings; it meant "setting himself up," in the true sense of the word, and acquiring both power and wisdom (*sapientia*). At the same time, however, concern for the continuity of the social structures ruled out the proliferation of new "houses," so that a mutation of such consequence was henceforth in store for only the few.

In the twelfth century the new behavior of those who gave sons and daughters in marriage stamped two new folds into the ideological garment overlaying the matrimonial practices. Divergent in appearance only, these two shifts in ideology were actually profoundly compatible and indeed complementary; moreover, they both adjusted to the major fault-line separating the youths (*juvenes*) from the elders (*seniores*) within aristocratic society. On the one hand, the new situation prompted the chivalric ideology to extoll the life of adventure more resoundingly than ever as a mock compensation for the frustrations of "youth." Here what is called "courtly love" came into its own. The sexuality of the bachelors had always been meandering. They freely availed themselves of peasant women, servant girls, and the many whores who were apt to relieve the champions of most of their winnings on the night after the tournament; they also took advantage of the widows whom they consoled and the "maidens" who so graciously received the heroes of the Breton romances at each nightly pause of their wanderings.[19] These bachelors were abductors by their very nature, for they were always tempted to take by force from another household the wife that would make them, at last, into elders (*seniores*). The code of the young extolled such triumphs over the control exercised by the elders, who alone had the power to bestow women. But now this dream of abduction was carried inside the very house that provided for the young men, into the house of the patron who gave them shelter, who "retained" them, and who every night went to bed with his own wife. The favors of the lady thus became the·stake in the competition among the bachelors of the court, a game that was similar in every point to the tournament, for it was aimed at attaining a mock capture that derived much of its excitement from flouting the strict prohibition of adultery and was tantamount to a kind of revenge against the common seigneur. The game of love was thus the expression of profound hostility to marriage. And yet it should be pointed out that it actually emphasized the importance of marriage, precisely because its objective was the breaking up of the married couple, because its rules demanded that the female partner be married, and because it observed the very social conventions imposed by the strategies of marriage itself. As Andreas Capellanus put it: "It is not proper to love a woman whom one would be ashamed to marry."[20] Above all, we must realize that when all was said and done, it was the elder (*senior*) who pulled the strings in this game. For he used these worldly rituals of social intercourse—and everyone knew that they were no more than that—for his own ends. By exhibiting his largesse to the point of letting his lady pretend that she was gradually giving herself, he was able to gain an ever stronger hold over the young men of his household, to domesticate them in the proper sense of that term.[21]

Domestication is the key word here. For, as another corollary to the structural strengthening of the lineage, aristocratic society now offered an alternative to dreams and games, holding out a new ideal to all the "youths" who, deep down, wanted only one thing, to be "young" no longer. It was the glorification of stability, the praise of the fruitful couple, temporarily entrusted with the husbanding of a patrimony by the deliberate choice of two families and engaged in legitimate procreation. At the very time when courtly eroticism was coming into its own, a powerful current of a different kind also began to take shape; but since literary historians have usually centered their attention almost exclusively on courtly love, we are apt to minimize the importance of this second current, although it too pervaded the entire literature of entertainment. Placing the married state at the pinnacle of a system of values, this current of thought exalted virginity for young girls, who were enjoined to preserve their sexual purity, reticence, and modesty before marriage. The same attitude which at that time led to greater differentiation between male and female attire also established different models of behavior for the two sexes: it was fitting for boys to be aggressive, but girls should be prudent and guarded.[22] It is easy to see that these two shifts discernible in the lay ideology were by no means contradictory. Their combined impact constituted a welcome aid in safeguarding what had now become, more clearly than ever, the keystone of the dominant society—the married state.

Once this model of matrimonial conduct had been crystallized, as it were, by the changes that took place within aristocratic society at the threshold of the twelfth century, it came into conflict with the model propounded by the Church, whose concern was not with the defense of earthly society, but with eternal salvation. I can treat the ecclesiastical model more briefly, since important scholarly studies, based on much more explicit sources, have cast a great deal of light on its structure.[23] This model was designed for the purpose of reconciling two contradictory exigencies. One of these was the reproductory function, with which God himself had endowed marriage when he instituted it in Paradise before the Fall as a continued act of creation and in order to fill his heaven with new denizens, since it was ordained that the order of the elect would henceforth replace the order of the fallen angels in all eternity. The other exigency was the need to curb the carnal impulses of human nature. The Church's profound loathing for sex was proclaimed by Odon of Cluny, for the Church saw sexuality as the principal means by which the Devil secured his hold on the creation. Quoting the Scriptures, the Church considered marriage a necessary institution and viewed it as the sacrament (*sacramentum*), the "sign," of the union between God and his creatures, between Christ and his Church. Nonetheless, the Church held that marriage was, if I may so express myself, a solution of last resort. Married persons (*conjugati*) were relegated to the lowest rank of perfection. Marriage was tolerated, but only as a remedy against carnal lust: after all, it was "better to marry than to burn" (*melius est nubere quam uri*). But, in any case, the only place for licit sexuality was within marriage. Beyond its confines, all sexual activity was fornication and, as such, cursed. Moreover, the physical act had to be strictly subordinated to the desire to procreate, and all pleasure had to be purged from it as much as possible. Hence, the

Church emphasized the union of two hearts in marriage and postulated that its validity rested more on the betrothal (*desponsatio*) than on the wedding, and especially on the consent (*consensus*) of the two individuals concerned. The Church thus unintentionally tended to take a stand against the power of the heads of households in matters of marriage, against the lay conception of misalliance, and, indeed, against male supremacy, for it asserted the equality of the sexes in concluding the marriage pact and in the accomplishment of the duties thereby implied. The rules decreed by the Church, in short, differed appreciably from the rules founded on the social code of morality. The ecclesiastical rules insisted on strict exogamy and monogamy. The Church's concept of incest had been excessive ever since the early Middle Ages, surpassing the prescriptions of Leviticus XIII and XX and extending the prohibitions to the seventh degree of consanguinity,[24] as well as to relationships by affinity and spiritual kinship. The Church condemned adultery, but judged it as severely in men as in women. It disapproved of remarriage for widowers and rigorously condemned repudiation.

The entire history of marriage in Western Christendom amounts to a gradual process of acculturation, in which the ecclesiastical model slowly gained the upper hand, not over disorder—as is too often claimed by those who blindly espouse the point of view of Churchmen whose testimony is almost all that has come down to us—but over a different order, one that was solidly entrenched and not easily dislodged. The real problem is not to find out why the victory of the ecclesiastical model was so slow and so precarious, but why this model was able to gain as much ground as it finally did. The fact is that the lay model was gradually infiltrated and eventually absorbed. The priests became involved in the marriage ceremony, adding certain acts of benediction and exorcism to all the solemn rites, whose climax they imperceptibly shifted from the house to the entrance gate of the church, and eventually to its interior.[25] The priests were also able to gain control over marriage by taking over its jurisdiction. This enabled them to institute reforms, to establish the rules, and to impose their own system of prohibitions. On the basis of the available source material, it is possible to outline two major phases in that long, drawn-out conflict.[26]

The first phase occupied the ninth century of the Carolingian age, when the actions taken by the bishops (and no longer by the monks) were in basic agreement with the policies of the sovereigns, and when a whole series of developments—such as the Council of Paris in 829, the labors of the moralists (*speculatores*), and the sanctions provoked by the marital difficulties of some of the greatest princes after 860—brought important victories to the ecclesiastical principles. As a direct continuation of the Carolingian program, the conflict then flared up again at the beginning of the eleventh century, in the very region of which I am speaking here. In this connection, I call your particular attention to the endeavors of Bishop Gérard of Cambrai, as set forth in the brief (*libellus*) against the heretics of Arras written at his behest in 1025.[27] In order to safeguard and, where necessary, reform the Church in the name of the discernment of the "orders" (*discretio ordinis*) or division between lay and ecclesiastical "orders," Gérard was fighting on two fronts. Steering a course, he said, between "two shoals," he attacked two opposing pronouncements; those of the heretics who, sustained by a broad current of radical spirituality, proclaimed the goal of frightening everyone, without distinction, from marriage (*omnes indiscrete a conjugiis exterrendo*) and those of the concubinary clerics who were in favor of enjoining everyone, without distinction, to enter into marriage (*omnes indiscrete ad connubia commonendo*). Gérard felt that discernment or division (*discretio*) commanded respect for two separate codes of behavior; the ecclesiastical man (*vir ecclesiasticus*) must not "become subservient to the marriage bed," while neither the Gospel nor the Apostle Paul prohibited marriage (*connubium*) to the layman (*vir secularis*), provided he knew how to avoid lust (*voluptas*), respected the times when sexual intercourse was forbidden, and cultivated the fear of God and the desire to beget children that would help him master the unruliness of his flesh.[28] (Note, by the way, that the bishop was only interested in the behavior of males.) Wedlock was therefore affirmed as the normal way of life for the laity. Here is the source of the Gregorian concept of marriage as an institution that we now understand so well, thanks to the work of Pierre Toubert.[29] Society was divided into two groups, namely, those who had chosen continence and served God in the Church, and the married people (*conjugati*) who served Him in the world, and who formed the core of the conjugal cell, the "house" that encompassed, regulated, and restrained those laymen who remained celibate by necessity rather than by choice. In conformity with this proposed program, a vigorous offensive was pursued throughout the eleventh century. Its agents were the bishops, whose resurgence, supported by the pope and his legates, made this struggle particularly intense in the two decades before 1100. It was during this period that the Church finally won the exclusive jurisdiction over all matters pertaining to marriage that it had long claimed as its right.[30] Henceforth, matrimonial disputes became the chief business of the episcopal courts.[31] The judges of these courts needed a normative tool, they needed juridical weapons, and they needed those compilations of canon law which, as Paul Fournier has said, had their "golden age" in the second half of the eleventh and at the beginning of the twelfth centuries.

At the threshold of the twelfth century, then, the confrontation was more acute than ever. Certain main points, it is true, were common to both models: both considered the household and the couple that formed its nucleus as the basic cell of lay society; both called for a solemn marriage ceremony as the sole means of establishing the legitimate character of the union and as a means of control; both condemned abduction and adultery; and both saw procreation or the engendering of nobility (*generositas*) as the purpose of marriage. On these points the two models actually reinforced each

20

other. Conflict, however, arose in three other areas; the "youths" were not about to give up pleasure or *joie* as the troubadours called it; those who had a son or daughter to marry were not about to give up their authority; and the married men were not about to give up the practice of repudiating their wives, any more than that of marrying their cousins. The lines of battle were clearly drawn. In the ensuing conflict, the Church fought from a position of strength, except on one point. And indeed, the resistance of the laity was quick to take advantage of a fissure that had developed within the ecclesiastical system as a result of the contradiction inherent in its insistence on both monogamy and exogamy. For while the Church proclaimed the indissoluble nature of marriage, it also decreed that any marriage in which the conjugal union was "sullied" by fornication or incest be dissolved.

The main issue in the conflict, then, was this precise point, which was also the point on which the Church modified its attitude in the course of the twelfth century, thereby opening the way to a gradual conciliation between the two models. Two principles, both essential to its doctrine, induced the Church to attenuate certain of its exigencies. On the one hand, the fact that they attributed decisive value to consent (*consensus*) between the spouses, to what we might call love, gave pause to the prelates when it came to dissolving a union based on the mutual understanding of two hearts, even if it was sullied by incest. On the other hand, the diversity of the patristic opinions, indeed the frequent contradictions among them, allowed them "sometimes to apply the full severity of the canons, sometimes to act with indulgence." In one respect only did the Church remain adamant: the decision was hers alone; she alone could decide whether the impediment of kinship should be invoked, in other words, whether the divorce should be "celebrated" or whether, by an act of grace, depending on the "quality of persons" and the circumstances of time and place, she might grant an exception, the dispensation (*dispensatio*).

II.

Incest, Bigamy,
and Divorce
among Kings and Nobles

The time has come to observe this battle. I feel that we must take a very close look, keeping track of the documents at all times. This is why I shall focus on some concrete cases, the clearest we have at our disposal. To this end, we must fasten our sight on the pinnacle of society, on bishops and kings. Especially on kings, since they served as examples and showed the people how to act. Moreover, the king's person was sacred, located as it was at the point of junction between terrestrial society and the celestial order, and therefore the object of the most watchful solicitude on the part of the Church leaders.

I shall begin with two letters addressed to King Henry I of England. Here the king was playing the role of giver in marriage for two of his daughters; the letters were written by two bishops, Anselm of Canterbury and Ivo of Chartres. Anselm was writing in response to a demand for advice.[1] The king had concluded a marriage agreement (*pactum conjugale*), promising one of his daughters to William of Warrenne, earl of Surrey, his comrade-in-arms at Tinchebray. Actually, this daughter was illegitimate, having been begotten in the course of his youthful wanderings, but she was of his blood and therefore a valuable asset, and the king meant to use her to strengthen a bond of friendship. Anselm, however, pointed out that the prospective spouses were cousins, one in the fourth, the other in the sixth degree, and thus could not be joined in marriage. Since "no pact can be kept against Christ's law" the king was urged to break it. Ivo of Chartres, for his part, took it upon himself to approach the king when a similar case arose.[2] This time, the king had ceded the hand of another bastard daughter to Hugh fitz Gervais, seigneur of Châteauneuf-en-Thimerais, who was among the parishioners (*parochiani*) of the bishop because of the property he owned in the region.[3] As soon as the betrothal (*desponsatio*) came to the attention of Bishop Ivo, he exhorted the king: His royal majesty cannot possibly allow an act that he is called upon to punish, Henry must not permit a marriage that will have to be dissolved on the grounds of incest.[4] To my mind, this letter is of particular interest for the following reasons: Ivo had at hand a "written genealogy," "drawn up by noble men issued from the same lineage, who are ready to count the degrees (*computare*) before the ecclesiastical judges and to prove them according to the law." Moreover, the bishop appends to his letter this genealogy beginning with the original trunk (*a tronco suo inchoata*), the "trunk" referred to being the (unnamed) father of Gonnor, the wife "by Danish custom" (*more danico*) of Richard I, count of the Normans. All of this proves that both prospective spouses are descendants of this common ancestor in the sixth degree, reckoning according to Peter Damian's *The Degrees of Consanguinity* (*De Gradibus Parentale*).[5]

This letter provides some very important insights. First of all, it shows that the genealogical memory vested in the males of the family was capable of reaching back six generations and, consequently, of embracing more than a century and a half. It also suggests that litigation of this kind stimulated the pursuit of genealogical information and that the need for written evidence gave it a fixed form. In its own way, the canonical impediment of consanguinity thus contributed to the strengthening of lineage-consciousness. Since beyond the sixth degree the genealogical memory began to slip, Alexander II, in his promulgation of a canon of the Council of Rome of 1059, advanced this very limitation as a justification for abolishing the incest prohibition beyond the seventh degree.[6] Yet even as it was, the kin-group affected by this prohibition was so widespread that the high aristocracy would have been totally ensnarled in the net of canonical impediments if it had complied with the ecclesiastical code.[7] That this had not been the case even forty years earlier[8] is shown by the genealogy that Ivo of Chartres sent to the king. Clearly, the clergy had strengthened its efforts to enforce these principles. The bishops asserted that any agreement concluded between the heads of two houses had to be broken if it violated them. Under these circumstances, divorce was not only legitimate, but indeed necessary.

And here are two other letters, also taken from Ivo of Chartres's correspondence. One of them was addressed, in 1104, to the papal legate, Hugh of Die, at the behest of Philip I, king of France.[9] The legate was asked to convene the prelates of northern France (*Francia*) at the next Christmas court, to hear a presentation of those who calculated the degrees (*computatores*) that would inform them that the marriage concluded seven years earlier between Philip's daughter Constance and Henry, count of Troyes, was tainted by incest—a very obvious incest that had certainly been well known at the time of the marriage pact, since the spouses were cousins in the fourth degree.[10] The marraige had to be annulled, and Constance was married, two years later, to Bohémond of Antioch. This case clearly demonstrates that when the Church was brought face to face with the contradictions inherent in its exigencies, it sacrificed the principle of indissolubility in order to preserve exogamy.

The second letter (ca. 1110)[11] directed the attention of the bishop of Sens to a projected marriage between the son of the count of Flanders and the daughter of the count of Redon, who were also cousins in the sixth and seventh degrees. This, the letter said, could be proven, indicating that here too the genealogical memory reached back to the middle of the tenth century.

Fortunately for us, Bishop Ivo was unable to attend the examination hearing and therefore forwarded the genealogical chart. The reason he is so well acquainted with the relationships within this family, he adds, is that "they have already been counted and proven at Pope Urban's court by the envoys of count Fulk of Anjou fifteen years earlier,[12] when they charged the king of France, Philip, with robbing the said count, his cousin, of his wife and unlawfully keeping her. As a result of these charges and of the proofs of consummated incest, the king was excommunicated by our lord Pope Urban at the Council of Clermont, whereupon the divorce became a fact."[13] This brings us to the "affair" on which I wish to concentrate, because it gathers together a whole cluster of indicative facts— the celebrated affair of Philip's divorce. Before going into any details, I must ask you to keep in mind that by 1110 Ivo of Chartres justified the king's condemnation for one cause alone, that of incest arising from a relationship of affinity.

The facts are well known.[14] In 1092, Philip I dismissed Bertha, the daughter of Gertrude of Saxony and the duke of the Frisians. He had married her in 1072, at the age of twenty, upon the advice of the count of Flanders, Gertrude's second husband. After a long period of barrenness, Bertha had borne him an heir, Prince Louis, in 1081.[15] While Philip was still in the process of getting rid of this woman, he appropriated another, Bertrade, at the time married to the count of Anjou and descended from the line of the seigneurs of Montfort,[16] a house that wielded great power in the province that had become the last stronghold of Capetian power. After their marriage, Philip and Bertrade were excommunicated three times, by Hugh of Die in 1094, by Urban II in 1095, and by the papal legate John at the Council of Poitiers in 1099. In 1104, Pascal II reconciled them with the Church. At Paris, Philip and Bertrade stood barefoot before the prelates of northern France and the abbots of the great Parisian monasteries and solemnly foreswore any conversation and companionship (*colloquium et contubernium*) between them.[17] I feel that it will be helpful to go over the sources for this story and to examine them very closely. These texts fall into three categories: charters, letters, and narratives.

The charters do not yield much. But there is one, dated by the lord of Beaugency "from the year in which Philip, king of France, married Bertrade, the wife of Fulk, count of Anjou."[18] Fulk of Anjou himself, in granting a charter in 1095, thought it appropriate to refer to France as "sullied by the adultery of Philip, her unworthy king."[19] The event thus found an echo in documents where one would never expect it to be reported. It is faint, to be sure, but it is there. This shows the repercussions of the scandal, for this marriage seemed truly extraordinary, involving nothing less than bigamy, "adultery" as Count Fulk himself said at the very time when his envoys stood before the pope to denounce the crime of incest.

The letters are much more explicit, especially those of Ivo, the newly elected bishop of Chartres, who had just sworn fealty to the king. Although his diocese largely escaped royal control, his church had close ties to Touraine and Anjou through its land. In 1092, Ivo asked the archbishop of Reims for advice.[20] Philip, he tells his correspondent, has just summoned him to aid in celebrating the marriage (*adjutor in celebrandis nuptiis*). Since it is not certain, however, that "the matter has been fully settled by apostolic authority and by the approval of the archbishop and his suffragans," Ivo refused to appear at the ceremony, "unless the archbishop is present as consecrator (*consecrator*) and performer (*actor*) of the wedding and his suffragans as advocates (*assertores*) and collaborators (*cooperatores*)." He adds that for certain reasons he is not free to disclose he cannot commend this marriage. As for the questionable "matter," we learn about it from another of Ivo's letters, addressed to Philip I himself.[21] Ivo starts out by asserting that in order to "settle" it, a general council will have to be held (and here the bishop of Chartres deliberately takes shelter behind papal authority); the council will have to decide, first of all—and this is clearly the first line of attack— whether the repudiation of Bertha is legitimate, and then whether the second marriage is legitimate. Unless this is done, Ivo refuses to meet the king's wife (*uxor*) in Paris (note that Bertrade is already considered his wife, and that the marriage ceremony is seen as the final consecration of the pact). As a jurist, Ivo is disturbed about this situation and tries to demonstrate to the king that he is not betraying his fealty, quite the contrary, for unless the legitimacy of this union is established, it will be harmful to the king's soul and to the crown. Later in the letter, he assumes the posture of the preceptor (*orator*), delivering an exhortation against carnal lust and the female peril, citing the examples of Adam and Samson, who were seduced by the woman (*mulier*), and of Solomon, who was so enthralled by his desire for women that he rebelled against his God.

Around the same time, Ivo wrote a response to the bishop of Meaux, who had solicited his advice.[22] The question put before him—Is it permissible for a man to take a concubine as his wife?—went to the very heart of the quandary facing the bishops of France (*Francia*), who were precisely called upon to legitimize an already consummated union through the rites of the Church. They earnestly debated the matter. Certain envoys of the Holy See were ready to adopt a lenient position; the legate Roger, for example, had told them that Saint Augustine permitted this and that local custom allowed it. In his letter, Ivo replies with a yes and no (*sic et non*) and puts together a small compilation of canon law. Against the proposition he invokes the authoritative texts of popes Gregory, Hormisdas, and Evaristus, as well as the councils of Châlon and Aix, which had condemned abduction.[23] In marshaling his authorities in this manner in order to formulate the prohibition, Ivo clearly calls upon several converging traditions: the ancient distinction of Roman law between companionship (*contubernium*) and matrimony (*matrimonium*), the unbending attitude toward pollution (*pollutio*) on the part of the more conservative prelates; and, finally, the Carolingian tradition which, in its concern for the preservation of social order, guaranteed the lineage's right to decide the fate of its daughters and punished abductors (*raptores*). Scrupulously honest, the bishop of Chartres also cites Augustine and Pope Eusebius who are in favor of consecrating such unions,[24] and then gives his own opinion.[25] Depending on the case, either indulgence or severity are called for; in the present case, he advises "not to commend the marriage (*conjugium*) before it takes place, and not to confirm it thereafter." In an attempt to win over the legate Roger, Ivo wrote him another letter concerning an analogous case in which he deferred again to papal authority, his main refuge.[26]

Meanwhile, Philip's wedding did take place. At this point, the pope decided to speak out.[27] Urban II lectured the archbishop of Reims, telling him that, like all the bishops of France except one—and we know who that was—he has been too accommodating; the bishop of Senlis has "with his own hands bestowed the priestly benediction" on the couple, thereby condoning the crime of "public adultery." A letter from Ivo of Chartres to Philip I[28] fills in the details. The pope has enjoined the king no longer to share the bed of the woman "he has taken as his wife," he will excommunicate him if he persists, and he has forbidden the bishops to crown this women with whom, as everyone on earth knows, the king is living in an unlawful manner. Let us sum up this second file of documents.

These letters demonstrate a number of points. They reveal that the betrothal (*desponsatio*), although it conferred the full status of wife (*uxor*) on the woman, and no doubt the sexual union (*commixio sexus*) also, were separate from the solemn wedding celebration. Nonetheless, everyone—and especially the king—was agreed that the Church's participation in this final ceremony was necessary. We also learn that the bishops of northern France (*Francia*) were willing to bless this marriage, and that only one of them, Ivo of Chartres, dissented and entreated his colleagues and the pope to follow his lead. He openly raised the issues of adultery, bigamy, or second marriage (*superductio*), and the crime of repudiating a wife without the confirmation of a duly certified divorce. And while he implicitly alluded to abduction, he never did so as long as Bertrade's husband was living, thereby indicating that in matters of this kind the entire blame was placed on the man. Finally, the letters make it clear that the pope could not make up his mind, and that when he finally excommunicated the king in person, probably at the Council of Clermont, it was on the grounds of incest, rather than adultery. This is exactly what Ivo of Chartres said in 1110, when, after Philip's death, he felt free to speak his mind.

As for the last category of sources, the narrative accounts, I shall divide them into three groups, according to how close in time they were to the event. Certain chroniclers spoke of it immediately, but did not say much.[29] They simply stated that Philip "abandoned" Bertha[30] in order to "take in marriage"[31] Bertrade, who, so far as they were concerned, became the queen.[32] One of the accounts mentions the ritual of consecration (*sacratio*) and—mistakenly—designates two bishops as the officiator (*operator*) and his assistant (*minister*).[33] As for the offense, the accounts allude to it only in connection with the excommunications. Upon the death of Bertha (1094)[34] Philip, who was no longer bigamous, convoked a council at Reims.[35] Hugh of Die, however, called another council at Autun, which decided that the king's bigamy was sufficient to warrant excommunication on the grounds that "during his wife's lifetime he took on another in addition (*alteram super induxit*)."[36] Then there was the matter of public adultery, which the chroniclers brought out in connection with the condemnation of Clermont.[37] Only one, the chronicle of Saint-Aubin of Angers, adds the accusation of incest—"for the crime of incest and adultery (*pro incesti adulterii crimine*)"[38]—but its writer was closest to Count Fulk and the whole controversy. And, of course, this chronicle presents the king to the world as a new David, the abductor of the wife of another man who, moreover, was his vassal.

The event is treated at greater length in the accounts composed during the third decade of the twelfth century, a great period in French and English historiography, and these accounts are inclined to discredit the late king, Philip.[39] They too show him as an abductor[40] and use this theme of abduction to build up a romance after the manner of the nascent chivalric literature, whose influence no chronicler in northern Europe could escape at that time. These chronicles devised their plots in various ways. As one would expect, the chronicle of the counts of Anjou[41] uses harsh words, calling the king lustful (*libidinosus*) and Bertrade the worst (*pessima*). She had always dreamed of being queen and, when she was seduced, she fled the conjugal chamber by night. William of Malmsbury essentially repeats the same thing. Bertrade left her husband, wantonly enticed by the greater name (*pruritu altioris nominis allecta*);[42] Philip had dismissed his first wife because she was too fat,[43] and he was inflamed with such ardor that he forgot the saying

> Majesty and love do not easily agree
> Nor dwell in the same seat.
> *Non bene conveniunt, nec in una sede morantur*
> *Majestas et amor.*[44]

love (*amor*) being virile desire. Ordericus Vitalis[45] also claims that it was not so much pride as lust (*voluptas*) that dominated the countess of Anjou. Afraid that she might have to share the fate of two previous wives (Fulk, left a widower by his first wife, had already repudiated two others) and be dismissed as a prostitute, she took the initiative herself and ensnared Philip, who was weak enough to consent to the crime and only then dismissed his "noble and saintly wife." Bertrade, that chameleon of a woman (*versipelis mulier*), was even able to reconcile her two husbands on the occasion of a banquet. Yet all these writers speak of a real marriage, of a betrothal (*desponsatio*) followed by a consecration (*consecratio*); both of them, of course, detestable.[46] As for the nature of the sin, no one had the slightest doubt that it was adultery, for which Philip was punished by "rotting" in his body.[47] Some of the chroniclers of the last third of the twelfth century still allude to the affair, but they only repeat, almost word for word, the accounts of the second generation.[48]

Now that we have closed the last of our files, one first fact is already clear. The men of the twelfth century viewed the union of Philip and Bertrade as a second marriage (*superductio*) following upon an act of repudiation that to Philip's contemporaries had been nothing more than a routine, habitual, and perfectly normal occurrence.[49] Yet we must inquire into the underlying reasons for the king's decision and, especially, for his fierce determination in resisting the repeated condemnations of the Church, which may actually have come as a surprise to him. It should be noted that in twenty years Bertha had given him only one son and that by 1092 there could be no doubt that she was barren. Recall, moreover, that at the time Philip was waging war against William Rufus, who, as Suger said, "aspired to the kingdom of France if, by some misfortune, this only son should die."[50] To protect the interest of the house whose head he was, Philip therefore changed wives and took Bertrade. She too was a descendant of Gonnor, and thus of Richard of Normandy, but her kinsmen, the Monforts and the Garlandes, no doubt pushed her into the arms of their seigneur.[51] She had amply proven her fertility and in due course was to contribute two more sons and one daughter to the Capetian line. It was vital, however, that these sons be considered legitimate. However "lecherous" he may have been—and how are we to know?—Philip therefore scrupulously observed the rituals: Bertrade was handed over and received a dower (*dos*),[52] and he solemnly celebrated his second marriage. His second wife became queen in the eyes of the world. Except, perhaps, in the eyes of Philip's son, the future Louis VI; and it is probably no coincidence that the "romance of Philip and Bertrade" took shape under his reign.

Immediately after his remarriage, Philip had been made to concede an appanage to his son Louis, and Bertrade was obliged to "repurchase" her dowry from the new king after the death of her second husband.[53] Moreover, when Suger, the official historiographer, spoke of Philip I's three sons, he made it very clear that Louis was born of the most noble spouse (*de nobilissima conjuge*) and the others of the second marriage with the countess of Anjou (*de superducta Andegavensis comitissa*); and when he spoke of the claims of William Rufus to the French crown, his narrative had already reached the years 1097–99, a time when Louis was no longer the "only son." His brothers, Philip and Florus, had already been born, but Suger added that "their succession was not taken into account."[54] All this explains why Philip was so adamant about keeping his second wife and why he was fighting so hard to have the legitimacy of this union recognized by everyone; but it also makes us wonder to what extent the whole affair was, if not altogether trumped up, at least inflated by those who surrounded the presumptive heir and, as Philip was growing older, spun their intrigues around Louis.[55] It was a case, then, of a domestic discord—a matter, in other words, concerning only the "house" itself—inflamed by a problem of doctrine.

This second issue, which no other French bishop considered, was raised by Ivo of Chartres, spurred on, perhaps, by the count of Anjou or even by the Norman adversaries of the Capetian king. It was then seized upon by Hugh of Die, who, with his customary zeal, was pursuing his reform, that is, his efforts to break down the resistance of the lay model. Finally, under prodding from Hugh of Die and Ivo of Chartres, Pope Urban II became involved. These rigorists began by condemning the "public adultery." Nothing was said about the woman who had left the bed of her living husband, and all the emphasis was placed on Philip's bigamy. This latter grievance disappeared in 1094. But even at that point the reformers, determined though they still were to dissolve the royal marriage, did not advance the argument of Bertrade's flagrant adultery, but instead turned to incest. This was their response to sharp criticism brought, not so much by Fulk le Rechin, count of Anjou, who apparently had little desire to take back Bertrade, as by Prince Louis, who was more sure of himself now that he had become his mother's heir and who saw young Philip's cradle standing in his way.

In 1096 the success of the Council of Clermont and the departure of Robert Curthose on the crusade, a fact that freed William Rufus to pursue his ambitions, further complicated the situation. These new involvements explain the imperious tone of the letters now written by Urban II to the archbishops of Sens and Reims against those bishops (among them the brand-new bishop of Paris, Bertrade's own brother) who had remained on good terms with the king and claimed that they could lift his excommunication without obliging him to leave his wife "because of whom We have excommunicated him."[56] They also explain the spurious acts of submission on the part of Philip I.[57] A last attack was mounted in 1099 by the Council of Poitiers —but we know that Duke William of Aquitaine, good vassal that he was, dispersed this council. In the absence of other clues to the laymen's thinking, this action tells us a great deal about the attitude they adopted toward this marriage, as long as it did not interfere directly with their own interests. Finally, five years later there was a reconciliation, largely encouraged by Ivo of Chartres,[58] in which everyone gave ground to some extent. What remained was the enduring memory of adultery. Yet behind this formal charge one clearly sees—and the literary accounts are very explicit on this point—only one really strong condemnation, that of the true pestilence, the contagion spread by woman, naturally faithless as she was. Henceforth, Bertrade was seen as the corruptress. As for Philip, he took his place in the collective memory as a weak, greedy man, the prisoner of his lust, much more the victim of seduction than a seducer, another Adam, another Samson, but definitely not another David. It was his misfortune that he lived at the precise moment when the tension between the ecclesiastical and the lay model of marriage was most acute, and that the man who stood in his way was Ivo of Chartres, the instigator of the Church offensive. Without him things would not have come to such a pass. And yet the point must be made that in his later years, by about

1110, Ivo no longer wanted to remember anything but the matter of incest. We shall see why.

Philip's marriage to Bertrade, like earlier, analogous cases of the ninth century, was an occasion for the leaders of the Church to define their position with respect to the matrimonial practices of the high aristocracy. To define it, but also to adjust it. There are indications that between 1092 and 1110 the ecclesiastical model underwent some imperceptible modifications. These we can follow in detail in the attitudes of Ivo of Chartres. Confronted with this scandal, as well as with other, similar cases, this bishop took a most intransigent stance in the early years of his episcopate. Yet he gradually relented, and not only because he was growing older, or because he wanted to protect his temporal interests in the face of the progressive penetration of Capetian power into his diocese. The unfolding of his thinking in this matter can be observed in another part of his correspondence.

Philip I's divorce had made Ivo the great authority in matters of marriage, and his colleagues, themselves struggling to resolve the difficult problems of pastoral guidance raised by the marriage strategies of great families, turned to him for advice. Most of the questions put before him involved the marriage of a fornicating woman, the regularizing of a concubinage—that is, one of the many unions concluded and consummated in the time-honored manner, beyond the control of the priests. This question had already been broached by the bishop of Meaux in connection with the king of France. It was raised again, more precisely, by Hildebert of Lavardin, the bishop of Le Mans:[59] What was one to think of a man who, by giving her his ring, concludes a marriage pact (*pactum conjugale*) with the woman who has shared his bed for many years? Ivo of Chartres replied that because "he has thereby performed the essential part of the marriage sacrament (note that it is man who performs the act, and that the sacrament [*sacramentum*], the sign of the conjugal union, is contained in the betrothal [*desponsatio*]) the union must not be broken, except in case of adultery" (and here he still stresses adultery, rather than incest).[60] Ivo ruled that this was a true marriage, that the conclusion of another marriage by one of the partners would constitute adultery, and that the man was not at fault, provided he became reconciled with the Church by adducing proof of mutual consent.

The case submitted by Odo of Orleans was similar:[61] Can a woman pregnant as a result of her fornication be lawfully married? Actually, however, it was more difficult to decide because, as Ivo noted in his reply, during her pregnancy and until the weaning of her child, no woman may lawfully make love, "without which the rights of marriage are not fulfilled." Nonetheless, the man must be commended for marrying the fornicating woman because he thereby returns her to chastity.[62]

These two statements by the bishop of Chartres attest to a complete reversal of the position he had taken in his response to the bishop of Meaux in 1092. Called upon to give thought to the matter of sanctifying illicit unions, Ivo was imperceptibly moved to consider the union of Philip and Bertrade in a different light.

This may explain his silence at the Council of Poitiers and his advocacy of indulgence even at that early date. The course of his thinking, which we can follow step by step, led him to stress indissolubility. This increasing emphasis on the union of two hearts, on consent (*consensus*) could only accelerate this evolution of his thinking. And indeed, Ivo of Chartres never ceased to stress the point that mutual consent was necessary and sufficient. This is what he told Bishop Humbold of Auxerre concernig the abduction of a girl already promised to another man.[63] She was abducted against her will, and the marriage was consummated. The girl wept and asserted that she had been forced. Ten men swore on her behalf; and the union was dissolved. The same reply was given to Hildebert of Le Mans, concerning another case:[64] In order to marry another woman, a man had broken a marriage pact, that is, a betrothal (*desponsatio*). Here again, Ivo ruled that a union with a girl who does not oppose her father's will must not be dissolved; what counts is the verbal agreement, which expresses the intention.[65]

Could it be said that Philip and Bertrade were not in agreement? Marriage, then, was indissoluble, except if "it is contracted without the consent of the partners, or if it is criminal in itself, that is, tainted by adultery or incest." In that case, the taint demands separation. Otherwise, whatever the vice infecting the spouses, whether it be abduction or excommunication, it must be tolerated in order to "preserve the conjugal faith."[66] Abduction will therefore not do as grounds for divorce, so that another of the charges leveled against Philip—

in an indirect way, to be sure—fell by the wayside. This left adultery and incest. Here Ivo was firm: "Fornication by the husband is grounds for divorce, in the same way as marriage with a cousin."[67] Yet when faced with concrete, actual cases, he retreated even here. In the case of certain crusaders (*Hierosolimitani*) whose wives had fornicated in their absence, he ruled that if they sought divorce, they should be forced to remain married.[68] Step by step, incest thus came to be the only grounds for divorce left,[69] the only lever by which the priests could hope to curb any aspect of the matrimonial behavior of the laity that distressed them.

Here is one last letter of Ivo's, written to the bishop of Soissons.[70] Peter fitz Gervais had married one of the daughters of Galeran of Breteuil, complete with betrothal (*desponsatio*) and priestly benediction, but he subsequently preferred to take this woman's sister. This, Ivo declared, is wrong, nor should it be objected that the marriage had not been consummated, for marriage is indissoluble as soon as the "pact" is concluded.[71] Moreover, and above all, the new marriage would be a case of incest by affinity, which has been condemned by the Church Fathers. It would seem that the gradual strengthening of such convictions was bound to result in Ivo's final attitude toward the second marriage of Philip I. It was indeed a true marriate, based on a legitimate pact between the king and his mistress (*pellex*). However, the pact was vitiated from within by incest, which is why divorce was a necessity. The Church did not yield. It continued to assert its competence over, even its power to control, the marriage strategy of the great lords. But it now placed the greatest emphasis on the canonical impediment of kinship. By shifting its line of attack, it unwittingly surrendered into lay hands a very strong weapon, capable of breaking down the obstacles which the Church's strict requirements concerning monogamy placed in the way of their schemes.

The controversy over Philip's double marriage, I am convinced, constituted the major turning point in the dialectic between two competing conceptions of the matrimonial order. This becomes even clearer, it seems to me, if we step back somewhat and consider a longer time span. I therefore propose that, once again, we avail ourselves of the light shed by the documents to examine, also in the Capetian lineage, two cases that pitted the Church leaders against the king. The first case is that of Robert the Pious, at the beginning of the eleventh century, the second is that of Louis VII, in the middle of the twelfth century.

There is no question that King Robert was polygamous, for he successively married three women, with the third marriage taking place immediately after the death of the first wife and while the second was still living. Here again, the facts are well known.[72] In 991–92, Robert repudiated Rosala, the daughter of King Béranger and the widow of the count of Flanders, a woman whom he had married three years earlier, when he was sixteen years old. Between 996 and the beginning of 997, he took as his new wife Bertha, the daughter of King Conrad, granddaughter of King Louis III, and the very recent widow of the count of Blois. He repudiated her in about 1004[73] in order to marry Constance, the daughter of the count of Arles and of the repudiated Queen Adelaide.[74] In 1009–10, he considered repudiating Constance in turn and remarrying Bertha,[75] but in the end decided against this step. In any case, he repudiated two wives and threatened a third. Let us now measure the repercussions of these various maneuvers in the medieval texts.

Richer, who in 996–98 furnished the main body of information on the first of these affairs, states that the "divorce" gave rise to some difficulties, but only because Robert did not want to give up the dower (*dos*) (the important castle of Montreuil-sur-Mer); he also indicates that certain churchmen, among them Gerbert of Reims, disapproved. Nonetheless, in reporting that the king married Bertha while his first wife was still living and that the marriage was solemnized by the archbishop of Tours acting as consecrator (*consecrator*), Richer does not breathe a word about "adultery." He only mentions the fact that Gerbert had advised Bertha against this marriage.[76] Some countercurrents were, however, stirred up. A reverberation of these can be perceived in a satirical poem written in 996 by Bishop Adalberon of Laon, who brought up the subject of incest.[77] His charge was not unfounded, for Robert and Bertha were cousins in the third degree. In fact, the celebration of this marriage had been forbidden by Pope Gregory V, cousin of Emperor Otto, shortly after his election (April 996), and in any case before the ceremony had taken place; and a year later the Council of

Pavia threatened to excommunicate King Robert and the bishops who had blessed this "incestuous marriage."[78] Greatly disturbed, the king entered into negotiations with Rome and dispatched Abbo, the abbot of Fleury, to Italy. On this mission, Abbo settled some matters pertaining to his own monastery in a most satisfactory manner, but in December 997 he too attempted, "at the risk of his life," to separate the royal couple. By the middle of the next year, the Council of Rome ordered Robert to leave his cousin, imposed seven years of penance upon him, and suspended the guilty archbishop and bishops until satisfaction was done.[79] This ruling had no effect whatsoever; Bertha peacefully continued to live with the king as his wife, the archbishop of Tours peacefully continued in his ministry, and Gregory V died. Robert eventually did separate from Bertha, but this was much later and for very different reasons. The fact is that the canonical impediment of a very close and very obvious consanguinity had been used to blackmail King Robert in the context of a tortuous diplomatic policy pursued by Emperor Otto and the papacy. The emperor was concerned that by his marriage to Bertha the king of France would introduce Carolingian blood into the house of Capet, and with it future claims to the kingdom of Burgundy. As for the papal diplomacy, it is evident that the steps taken by Pope Gregory and by Abbo of Fleury were directly related to the synod of Saint-Basle of Verzy (991), to the discord sown by the deposition of Archbishop Arnulf of Reims and his replacement by Gerbert among the French bishops, and to the fierce struggle the monks of Cluny and Fleury were waging in order to be free from episcopal supervision. For the pope and those monks who relied on him, attacking Robert on his marriage was an excellent means of wresting concessions in another area from the king and his episcopate. And indeed, this strategy brought results.[80]

Still, the attack was not without effect on Robert's later conduct; he eventually did repudiate his second wife. There are reasons to believe that pangs of conscience were indeed involved in the conduct of a king who was gradually becoming "monkified"—an attitude for which he was severely criticized by Adalberon of Laon sometime before 1030. This supposition is bolstered by the very discreet account of this matter written by Helgaud. A monk of Fleury also, but definitely not a supporter of Abbo, Helgaud had very little sympathy for Queen Constance when, between 1031 and 1044—long after the event—he wrote his altogether hagiographical eulogy of the late king. Even he could not avoid charging the king with the very sin of David and with offending God by taking as his companion a woman who was forbidden to him on two counts, since she was not only his cousin but also a godparent with him of the same godchild. Nonetheless, Helgaud praises the king for effacing his wrongdoing by breaking this union and by doing penance;[81] indeed, the allusion to the sin, placed at the very middle of the account, is but the introduction to the crucial passage, which describes the royal contrition.

The plain fact is, however, that Robert only affected to yield to the Church's injunctions because the well-founded charge of incest permitted him to change wives once again by 1004, and in the most legitimate manner. This second divorce also served the interests of the Capetian house. We must realize that in this new dynasty the most urgent problem was the consolidation of a dubious and contested legitimacy by means of blood and marriage alliances. As a first step it was important not to compromise one's station by taking wives from the rank (*ordo*) of vassals, but to choose the daughters of kings, which Robert always did. From this point of view, his third wife was actually the least valuable asset, even though her mother had been the wife of the last Carolingian sovereign. Although abandoned, she had been a duly crowned queen. As a result, the history writers of the thirteenth century, such as Gervais of Tilbury, were to designate Constance as the principal factor in the dynastic transfer of 987, describing her as the daughter of Louis V and claiming that she, along with the kingdom, had been ceded to the son of Hugh Capet.

Marrying the daughters of kings, however, was worth doing only if they produced male heirs. Is this why Robert took the precaution of marrying a succession of widows who were positively known not to be barren? By this criterion, though, Rosala was too old, and Richer tells us that this is why he dismissed her. Bertha was not quite so old and had already borne at least four children, but then the years went by and her new husband did not make her pregnant. After seven years the king, tired of waiting and deeply concerned, dismissed her in turn, and I am convinced that it was for this pressing reason. He now took a virgin, who immediately gave him two sons. Once this was taken care of, he was strongly tempted to return to his previous wife. At this point, other factors intervened, among them the intrigues of the court and a new and equally urgent problem confronting the Capetian kings, namely, the need to oppose a ground swell of forces that was creating everywhere in *Francia* strong principalities that confronted the royal domain. On the Flemish and Norman flanks it was already too late. But the game was not yet over, around the year 1000, in Anjou and in the region of Blois, whose counts were locked in rivalry and whose supporters were pitted against each other even in the royal entourage.[82] The Capetians could also hope to hold out in the region of Chartres and in Touraine. The marriage between Robert and Bertha took its place within this strategy: In 996, immediately upon the death of the count of Blois who had left minor children, and at the very moment when Fulk Nerra, who had defeated him, made his entry into Tours, the archbishop of that city solemnly united the widow of the deceased count with the king of France, who immediately reconquered Tours and took the sons of his new wife under his tutelage.[83] This explains why Fulk Nerra was among those who lined up behind Abbo and attacked this marriage in 998. The same Capetian policy prompted the divorce of 1004.

At the time when Robert was making plans to take over his Burgundian heritage, Bertha's son Odo, having reached his majority, became count of Blois and was released from the royal guardianship. At that point,

Robert changed wives and married Constance, a cousin of the count of Anjou. This marriage had resulted not only from an intense dynastic preoccupation but also from a reversal of alliances. The reversal was not altogether firm, however, since Odo and his mother continued to wield great influence within the royal house. In fact, their influence was so strong that in 1008 Fulk Nerra felt it necessary to have his men assassinate the count of the palace Hugh of Beauvais, a member of that coterie. Hence we hear of "Bertha's furtive returns to favor,"[84] and the marital crisis around 1010. Bertha stepped up her efforts to return to the royal bed; meanwhile the French bishops were becoming restive, partly as a result of the struggle over monastic exemption, a matter that in a sense was further aggravated by the difficulties the implantation of Capetian power was encountering in Burgundy.[85] Was Robert about to undertake yet another divorce? He returned from Rome determined to adhere faithfully both to his new alliances and to his new wife. This attitude, in turn, triggered the break with Odo of Blois and the long, drawn-out confrontation that ensued.

One last offensive against Queen Constance was mounted, however, in 1022. At that time the heresy of Orleans was raging. The royal entourage was in the throes of a violent purge, instigated by the ecclesiastics of the region of Chartres, who were quite evidently manipulated by Odo of Blois. The victims of the purge were the queen's closest friends. They were very cultured men of the highest spirituality who, with respect to marriage, professed an attitude that deserves our special attention. Reticent about sacramental gestures of any kind, they disapproved of the Church's involvement in the profane rites of marriage (*conjugium*). To them, marriage was a carnal, and hence, contemptible matter; they felt that it should be left to the laity and not be mixed with the sacred. They thus gave very free rein to the tortuous negotiations leading up to the conclusion of marriage alliances.[86] What is important here is the evident weakness at that time of the ecclesiastical model by comparison with the vigor of the lay model. The cluster of events I have attempted to reconstruct from the faint traces they have left strikingly illustrates the freedom to repudiate and the power of endogamic practices within the high aristocracy. Only Rome and a few "purists" were brandishing interdicts against these practices. But, on the one hand, they did not put too much faith in the effectiveness of their intervention, and, on the other hand, they used it to further their own policies. Contrary to what was believed by certain nineteenth-century erudites and by the historical genre-painters who took their inspiration from them, King Robert was never excommunicated. What bishop would have dared to do this? No one condemned him, except those who had a grudge against him—and Helgaud tells us that it was in order to silence them that he touched upon the marital disorders in the life of his hero. Ralph Glaber did not breathe a word about them, even though he was ordinarily much interested in such matters.

The accounts of a condemnation were written much later, at the time when the ecclesiastical offensive was gathering momentum and opened the way for Ivo of Chartres's campaign. Who denounced King Robert as incestuous? Who depicted him as punished by Heaven, showing that his guilty copulations had engendered a monster ·with the neck and the head of a goose? Who said that almost all the bishops of Gaul had excommunicated him and that he was shunned by all his family like a man stricken with the plague, until he finally consented to a divorce and returned to a legitimate marriage? Why, it was Peter Damian, that vehement reformer, who concocted his wild stories and wielded his raging pen under the reign of Philip I. His indictment was reiterated, almost word for word, in the fragment of a history of France ending in 1110.[87] Now 1110 was the exact moment when Ivo of Chartres himself, a bit wiser, and satisfied with a partial victory, began to bring up the matter of incest. Indeed, it was the moment that I consider the main turning point in this long history. These two texts are proof that the Church had won. But the victory came late, and it must be emphasized that it came about because in this phase of the struggle the Church imperceptibly gave some ground in the matter of bigamy in order to concentrate its attack upon incest. Why? Was it because endogamy was the weak spot of the lay ethos, the chink that no doubt opened the mind of the laity to the idea of a taint, to pangs of conscience, and to the equally persistent feeling that consanguineous unions were bound to produce monstrous offspring? Or was it because, in a very concrete manner, the unavoidable incidence of incest led to a profusion of disputes in which the Church and its judicial system felt called upon to intervene and act as arbitrator? However that may be, it was a victory, but how long would it last? Let us turn from the grandfather to the grandson of Philip I, to Louis VII.

His divorce had a political impact of such importance that historians have written a great deal about it, although most have missed the point. This is why, here again, we must attentively reread the sources. Let us start with a text which, although written relatively late—thirteen years at the earliest after the event—is an official document and part of the royal historiography. I am referring to the "History of Most Illustrious King Louis VII" (*Historia gloriosissimi regis Ludovici VII*), whose author was a monk who had moved from Vézelay to Saint-Germain-des-Prés. With some revisions, this text was inserted into the continuations of Aimoin. Molinier dates it from 1171, but he probably attaches too much importance to a few passages that may well have been recast at a later date. I wonder whether, in fact, the birth of Philip Augustus on 21 August 1165 was not the occasion for this tribute to King Louis VII. We know with what relief this event was greeted in Paris, and we also know that it was celebrated as the reward for the "works of justice" accomplished by the father. In any case, the account dwells at considerble length on the most solemn baptism of the newborn;[88] indeed the entire narrative, particularly in its treatment of the divorce, is conceived with a view to this providential birth, to this blessing bestowed upon the lineage of the kings of France while the lineage of the kings of England was, not without reason, deprived.[89] At the very beginning of his work, immediately after a passage that Molinier considers to be the fragment of an unfinished work by Suger, the monastic author mentions Louis VII's first marriage.[90] He describes the events of the crusade without the slightest allusion to any marital difficulties, indeed relating the holy voyage to the birth of a second daughter. Then, having treated Henry Plantagenet's installation as duke of Normandy, he devotes a chapter to the divorce (21 March 1152). According to him, the initiative for the separation came from the king's kinsmen, who approached him to demonstrate that his wife was his cousin and were willing to prove it by oath (and it is true that Louis and Eleanor were related in the fourth and fifth degrees respectively; a fact that was apparently known to everyone at the time of the marriage in 1137). Counting and then swearing: by now we are well acquainted with the procedures that were followed.[91] Unable to tolerate the thought of continuing to live in sin, the good king took care of the matter in the most judicious manner. He turned to the archbishop of Sens, the prelate whose "parishioner" he was, and asked him to convoke a council at Beaugency, which formally declared the incestuous union null and void.[92] Set free, Eleanor married Henry of Normandy without delay (*sine mora*).[93]

In exemplary fulfillment of his duties as the head of a house, Louis VII now concluded the best possible marriage pacts for his two daughters[94] and then proceeded to remarry himself. At this point, the author of the *Historia* feels called upon to justify this second marriage, this bigamy. To this end, he refers to two moral codes, the divine code, which enjoins man to take unto himself a wife, and the dynastic code, which obliges the king to give an heir to the kingdom of France.[95] In 1154, then, Louis VII married the daughter of the Emperor of Spain and immediately set to work. However, he was only able to beget another daughter (who was soon betrothed [*desponsata*] to the very son of Eleanor and Henry, although it was necessary to take every possible precaution, and indeed to seek the consent of the Holy See, since here the impediment of kinship was very strong).[96] Later, a second daughter was born, who cost her mother's life. Five weeks later[97]—the king was pressed for time, he was forty years old—he took a third wife, urged on, his biographer tell us, "by the bishops and the other barons." The same two reasons are given to justify such impatience to remarry. The king acted as much "for his salvation"—obsessed by Saint Paul's word: "It is better to marry than to burn"—as for "the protection of the common weal," "fearing that the kingdom of France might come to be ruled by an heir not issued from his seed."[98] Here the ecclesiastical model, the concept of marriage held at Saint-Germain-des-Prés, appears in full light. The marital state is the normal way of life for a layman, a naturally concupiscent creature who, moreover, is obliged to perpetuate his house.[99] That goal the king pursued with great assiduity, although it took him five years to make his young wife pregnant.

Clearly, the account of divorce [in the *Historia*] is used to advance the "plot" culminating in the birth of the future king. But this text also reveals the true motive for the rupture, the one thing that is never mentioned by anyone. After fifteen years of marriage, Eleanor had presented the Capetian lineage with nothing but girls. Yet the separation was perfectly legal, duly authorized, because of incest, by the Church, which consecrated the two subsequent remarriages with the utmost solemnity.[100]

Let us now confront this very official account of the divorce with the other testimonies. Four of these were written earlier. I wonder whether the one account that is chronologically closest to the event was not originally part of the "Annals of Cambrai" (*Annales cameracenses*) of Canon Lambert, who wrote this passage in 1153. Here Louis VII is not judged, except for his "puerility"; but he is blamed for listening to bad advice, and the beginning of the marital discord is pushed back to the voyage to the Holy Land.[101] Writing at the same time, Henry of Huntingdon too looks at the matter from the political standpoint, is very careful not to pass judgment, and confirms the involvement of those who swore to the kinship.[102] Ten years later, Richard the Poitevin (Pictavensis), a close associate and admirer of Bishop Henry of Blois, and consequently hostile to the Plantagenets, included the praise of Louis VII in his *Universal Chronicle*. He criticizes the king for only one thing, a moral shortcoming, namely, for removing his first wife from his bed and so quickly taking another. The most interesting aspect of this appraisal is the fact that Richard, a Cluniac monk, feels that those responsible for the divorce were not the king's family, but Pope Eugenius III, Bernard of Clairvaux, and Bishop Geoffrey of Langres—in other words, the Cistercian party. The royal divorce, he says, just like the second crusade, resulted from the pernicious influence of the White Monks (Cistercians).[103] More garrulous, John of Salisbury in his *History of the Popes* (*Historia Pontificalis*) (1161–63), a work dedicated to the Cistercian Peter de la Celle and presenting the views of the Roman clergy, places this divorce into a much clearer and altogether different light.

1. Eleanor had taken the initiative when she was at Antioch, where her uncle, the count, had ensnared her in the game of courtly love.[104] Not eager to follow her husband to Jerusalem, it was she who advanced the argument of kinship in the fourth and fifth degrees, since she was sure that Louis VII would be sensitive to it.[105] Louis, lacking maturity, was bewitched by his wife,[106] but he also listened to certain persons in the royal entourage who, like the *losengiers* of chivalric literature, denounced the flightiness of the lady and planted in the king's mind the seeds of fear that she might desert or dishonor him.[107]

2. Long before the royal couple went overseas, their kinship relation was already openly discussed in France. Eleanor based her argument on a statement of Bishop Bartholomew of Laon (1112–53), who had publicly counted the degrees some years earlier in another divorce case.[108]

3. When the royal spouses were passing through Italy on their return from the Holy Land, Eugenius III

intervened vigorously, but with the aim of preventing a separation. As an astute politician, this pope chose to treat an obvious case of incest with indulgence in order to safeguard the indissolubility of marriage.[109] He made the husband and wife sleep together (which qualms of conscience had no doubt prevented Louis VII from doing), solemnly prepared a bed to that effect,[110] confirmed the union, blessed the couple—it was almost like a second wedding—and exhorted them to live united, not by *amor*, that is, concupiscence, but by *caritas* (divine love). He was so convincing that Eleanor soon gave birth to another child, unfortunately a girl.

As you can see, none of these four accounts mentions the Council of Beaugency. They all speak of the divorce as of a wrong, instigated by the nefarious advice of intimate friends within the royal house.

At this point of the investigation, I shall turn to two more direct sources. They are two letters. One was sent by Saint Bernard to the Cistercian Cardinal Stephen of Preneste[111] long before the divorce (it was written in 1143), but at the time of another divorce that served the interests of Louis VII—a case that I shall discuss in detail later. Referring to the king, Bernard writes to the cardinal: "How does this man dare to advance the argument of consanguinity when he himself is living openly with his cousin," "his cousin in the third degree"[112] (as usual the abbot of Clairvaux is exaggerating). The other missive reached Louis VII in the Holy Land; its author, Abbot Suger, mentions "the sovereign's resentment toward the queen" and recommends patience.[113]

Let us return to the chronicles, but to much later ones. The echo they reverberate testifies not so much to the events themselves as to their repercussions in high society. In a brief and impartial account, Robert Du Mont limits himself to relating the preliminary estrangement, the legitimate separation at Beaugency, the queen's rapid remarriage, and the steps taken by Louis VII to defend the rights of his daughters. Robert thus very closely follows the *Historia gloriosissimi regis Ludovici VII*.[114] By contrast, William of Tyr, writing in the Holy Land, corroborates the *History of the Popes* (*Historia Pontificalis*). He attributes the entire responsibility to the count of Antioch, saying that it was he who, playing upon the natural folly of woman, enticed Eleanor away from her duty.[115] At the turn of the twelfth and the thirteenth centuries, the very heyday of the rivalry between the kings of France and the Plantagenets, references to the event become more and more frequent in the texts which, I believe, can be separated into three groups.

Some very wordy texts were written in England. William of Newburgh, favorably disposed to Henry II and closely tied to the Cistercians, makes much of the weakness shown by Louis, who behaved like a "youth" rather than like an elder (*senior*), burning with excessive love for Eleanor's lovely body. He set a bad example by not leaving her behind when he departed overseas, for under these circumstances he could not hope to enforce chastity among the crusaders and thus precipitated the failure of the venture. As John of Salisbury had done, William squarely places the responsibility for the marital crisis upon Eleanor. Not that he accuses her of adultery, but, as he says, she was too passionate and therefore complained that "she had not married a king, but a monk." Henry Plantagenet was made of different stuff; he attracted her, and she regained her freedom, easily overcoming the feeble resistance of the Capetian king.[116] Gervais of Canterbury, on the other hand, was hostile to the Plantagenets; he veiled his face in horror and reported all manner of gossip. As far as he was concerned, the divorce was most legitimate, solemnly celebrated before the Church (*in facie ecclesiae*), but based on false grounds and specious oaths. He was convinced that the consanguinity was no more than a pretext for Eleanor, and especially for Henry, who was enthralled by the pedigree of the woman (*generositas feminae*) and even more by the desire to lay his hands on Aquitaine.[117] The most violent attack against the king's wife was made by Gerald of Wales. He could never forgive this new Melusine for contaminating the race of English kings with the germ of perversion;[118] moreover, her second union was doubly adulterous, for had not Henry's father already briefly possessed her?[119] The other accounts are much shorter. Some, like the *Continuation of Anchin*, follow the tradition hostile to Saint Bernard;[120] other, Cistercian, authors are as passionately opposed to Eleanor as the English writers: According to Helinand of Froidmont, Louis was justified in dismissing this woman for her licentiousness, for she "did not behave like a queen, but rather like a whore."[121]

But in any case, all the sources are agreed on one point: the divorce was wrong; above all, in a period dominated by the sudden rise of independent states, it was politically wrong. All the sources attempt to explain, if not to justify it. In this endeavor, they pursue three divergent directions. At the court of France, no one had any doubt: Louis VII acted for the salvation of his soul and in the interest of the kingdom. Those authors who faithfully followed the Cluniac line felt that the king had received bad advice and fell victim to Cistercian machinations. To all the others, the Cistercians and the English chroniclers, who could not help seeing the event as it was seen at the courts of Henry II, where the pervasive ethos of courtly romance had reached its highest pitch, the fault was all Eleanor's, a graceful, fickle woman who made sport of a too eager husband. Yet with all those whose testimony has come down to us—except one, the official historian of Louis VII—the matter of consanguinity counted for very little. They considered it an argument that was seized upon in order to legitimize a necessary repudiation. True value lay in the indissolubility of marriage.

Scaling the heights of the social hierarchy is a necessity in this undertaking, although it does allow us to observe the personalities who were supposed to be mirrors of perfection. In addition, however, it seems to me that this is much the best vantage point from which to follow the stages in the competition between the two concepts of marriage. During the first half of the eleventh century the propensity of the high aristocracy for repudiating wives and choosing them from among the close kin-group does not seem to have encountered any obstacles. Except, that is, when the Church—

and more precisely the segment of the Church that looked to Rome—felt that it was to its own advantage to thwart this matrimonial strategy. The Gregorian restoration of the episcopacy; the principle of the distinction of the orders (*distinctio ordinum*) underlying the reform projects undertaken by the pope, the papal legates, and those of the bishops who followed them; the efforts to extend the competence of the ecclesiastical jurisdictions; the intense scrutiny of the normative texts that added fuel to the struggle; and the very sincere desire on the part of many churchmen to rescue worldly society from sin—all these were factors that focused the struggle between spiritual and temporal values upon the institution of marriage by the last third of the eleventh century.[122] One of the Church's champions was Ivo of Chartres. I feel that he must be considered the designer of the dogmatic edifice constructed after 1110 by the commentators of the Bible (*divina pagina*).[123] The more clear-cut distinction between the betrothal (*desponsatio*) and the marriage (*nuptiae*) formulated by Bishop Ivo when he was faced with practical problems is at the root of the subsequent propositions by Anselm of Laon, William of Champeaux, and Peter Lombard concerning the two "faiths" (*fides*), agreement and consent, and the two promises given for the "future" and in the "present." It was only because ever-increasing value was placed on words (*verba*) and consent (*consensus*) that Hugh of Saint-Victor could make mutual consent the key to licit wedlock, the greatest sacrament (*majus sacramentum*), a sign of the ineffable union between the soul and

God.[124] Yet in an insidious way, this orientation of theological thinking and the canonical measures that proceeded from it tended to be harmful to both of the conflicting models. Harking back to what Abelard had said about individual responsibility and the spiritual equality of men and women, such thinking blunted the cutting edge of the Church's instruments of control, for its traditional principles—as well as its age-old suspicion of female depravity—made the solemn celebration of marriage mandatory as a means of conducting more rigorous investigations of cases of incest and adultery. And the new attitude was even more threatening to the authority of the heads of houses, for it lent fuel to the demands of the youths (*juvenes*) and their "bel amour" by exalting the lovers' choice that was one of the tenets of courtly love. It also opened the door to excessive claims. Here for instance is the monk Henry who in 1116 at Le Mans attacked everything in the conclusion of a marriage pact that might stand in the way of the agreement of two hearts—money, family interest, but also the Church's ritual and the canonical impediments it was determined to enforce.

At least the new theology established the supremacy of indissolubility, of that stability (*stabilitas*) which, according to Hildebert of Lavardin, [125] constitutes the very foundation of the sacrament, since it is the sign of a sacred thing (*signum sacrae rei*), of the mystical union between Christ and his Church. Because Ivo of Chartres had recognized that the mutual giving of two persons had the power to cleanse them of the stains of the sin of the flesh, he had come to allow that a man could legitimately take his concubine as his wife, and that the Church could not refuse its benediction to couples who had become united by their own free will; an attitude that also induced him to close his eyes to the bigamy of Philip I. Henceforth, Ivo could only charge the king with committing incest. As a result of this change in emphasis, pastoral guidance as practiced in the second third of the twelfth century came to subordinate the purification of unions sullied by adultery or incest to the stability of the conjugal union. This is what Eugenius III did when faced with the discord between Louis and Eleanor. The Church thus imperceptibly shifted its line of attack against the practices of the laity. Henceforth it fought for the permanence of the marriage unit. This shift was to produce a remarkable inversion. In the past, the canonical impediment of consanguinity had usually been raised by the priests in order to break marriages they considered bad. Henceforth, it was raised by the laymen if they wanted to recover their freedom and restore fluidity to their marital commitments. This reversal should be demonstrated by additional cases. I shall adduce only one example here and will therefore discuss another divorce case, one that was actually closely related to the divorce of Louis VII. This was the conflict between the Church authorities and Ralph of Vermandois, senechal of France and first cousin to the king.

In 1142, Louis VII, acting as the head of his lineage, had decided to give in marriage to Ralph of Vermandois a sister of his own wife, unconcerned about any imped-

iment on the grounds of affinity, and even less concerned about the more serious fact that Ralph was already married. Ralph repudiated his wife, advancing
the argument of consanguinity. Our principal source
for this affair is the abbot of Saint-Martin of Tournai,[126]
Herimann, who before 1146 related the beginning of a
very long story. We only hear about it by chance,
because the matter happened to concern him in a
rather personal way. Hoping to take advantage of the
fact that the bishop of Noyon, Ralph's brother, was
suspended—precisely because he had lent a hand in
this divorce—Herimann had tried to persuade the
pope to install a bishop at Tournai. At Rome, where the
matter was debated, the candidate to this episcopal see
had failed to appear, fearing that he did not have
enough money to gain support among the members of
the Curia; but the bishop of Noyon was there, with his
pockets full of money. For five hundred silver marks he
obtained his reinstatement, and the monks of Tournai
were again placed under his rule. Herimann's resentment led him to talk about still another scandal.

The bishop of Noyon, the bishop of Senlis, and
Bartholomew, the bishop of Laon, whom we have encountered already, had solemnly dissolved Ralph's
first marriage on the faith of witnesses who, the abbot
of Tournai claims, had counted wrongly and perjured
themselves. And indeed, one wonders if the senechal
could have been closer to his first wife than to his
second, to whom he was related in the third and fifth
degrees. All might have ended well if the family of the
repudiated wife had not suddenly balked, led on by an

uncle, the most powerful male of the lineage, Count Theobald of Champagne.[127] At that point, the matter became inflamed by old grudges, many of them stemming from the Anacletan schism that pitted the Capetian house, the house of Aquitaine, and the monks of Cluny against Innocent II, Saint Bernard and one prince whom the abbot of Clairvaux controlled and manipulated as he saw fit, namely, Theobald of Champagne. In 1138, and again in 1141, Theobald had refused to serve his seigneur in Aquitaine. Why? 1138 and 1141 were precisely the dates when in one case the election of the bishop of Langres and in the other that of the archbishop of Bourges had led to violent quarrels between Louis VII and Saint Bernard.[128] Now the matter of Ralph's divorce arose only a year after the latter of these conflicts. Saint Bernard, vehement and excessive as usual, and capable of every chicanery, decided to join the melee. He saw this case as a way to attack the king of France in a weak spot, in order to oblige him to let Peter de la Châtre ascend the archepiscopal see of Bourges.

The letters dispatched in every direction by the abbot of Clairvaux are enlightening to us. In writing to the pope, he voiced support for the charge brought by Theobald of Champagne that Ralph had been married by the ministers of the Church, that is, by God, from whom they held their power. How dare anyone break this union and, worse yet, by means of money?[129] Against the presumption of incest, Saint Bernard thus stresses the principle of indissolubility, which shows that he was in the mainstream of the ecclesiastical thinking of his day. And indeed, the Council of Langres, convoked by the papal legate—like the Council convoked one and a half centuries earlier by Gregory V to deal with Robert the Pious—enjoined Ralph under penalty of excommunication to break with his new wife and condemned the three bishops as guilty of condoning this bigamy. But then Louis VII took up arms, compelled Theobald to accept the divorce, and made him promise to have the decision of Langres annulled. And indeed, Ralph was absolved. At that point, Saint Bernard returned to the charge, urging Innocent II to confirm the condemnation of the "adulterous tyrant"[130] and to renew the anathema against him.[131] He also advised Theobald to resist the king by similar means, that is, to pursue an adverse marriage policy. Additional conflicts therefore ensued when the count of Champagne concluded marriage pacts with the count of Soissons and with the count of Flanders, giving a daughter to the former and receiving a daughter from the latter.[132] The Capetian king saw such agreements as a breach of the fidelity to which he was entitled. Here we see the first sign of a mutation in the lay model of matrimonial practices that was taking place in northern France at that time, namely, the usurpation of the right to control the dynastic strategies of his vassals by the feudal seigneur. In order to dissolve the Flemish marriage, Louis VII invoked, moreover, the usual pretext, consanguinity. The spouses, he points out, were related in the third degree.[133] At this juncture, Saint Bernard wrote the already cited letter to Stephen, cardinal-bishop of Preneste.[134] It testifies to the growing role of the College of

Cardinals in matters of this kind, for henceforth it was necessary to seek allies among the members of the Curia, to convince, seduce, and buy them. Saint Bernard's letter is a violent indictment of the king of France: "In his customary manner, he has forced the bishops to bless what should be cursed, curse what should be blessed"; in order to overcome their resistance, he has moved heaven and earth to find "swearers who would use perjury to separate by human means those who are united by God." Here Saint Bernard's conception conforms even more clearly to the theology of marriage that had just been elaborated by Hugh of Saint-Victor and the other commentators of Scripture: Consanguinity is a concern of men, a concern of the flesh, while indissolubility is a concern of God; which is why the impediment of consanguinity cannot be brought to bear against the obligation of stability (*stabilitas*). Bernard does not want to hear about incest. He knows only one thing: to forbid the conclusion of this marriage would be to deprive the Church of her weapons, and those who mean to do this must be considered as true schismatics.[135] Here he reveals the real reasons for his stance, those that in his opinion should guide the attitudes of the Church leaders. He feels that they can permit incestuous marriages not only from the dogmatic point of view, since the sacred nature of consent (*consensus*) prevails over anything related to kinship, which is merely a matter of blood, a matter of the flesh, but also whenever the interest of the Church is at stake.

Once Celestine II succeeded Innocent in September 1143, the storm abated. The sanctions levied against the king of France were lifted, and Theobald of Champagne was encouraged to break the two marriages he had contrived as a counteroffensive. But the case of Ralph remained pending. It was discussed, inconclusively, at Corbeil and then, in the spring of 1144, at Saint-Denis, where Bernard was said to have promised Eleanor an end to her barrennness if she would give better advice to her husband. This she must have done, for a year later she gave birth to a second daughter. (When this daughter, incidentally, was promptly betrothed to Henry Plantagenet [1146], it was Saint Bernard who objected on the grounds of an impediment of kinship—but then this was not the first or the last time that he contradicted himself.)[136] Ready to leave on the second crusade, the count of Vermandois tried to secure confirmation of his union, but was made to wait for some time. The matter was finally settled, six years after his remarriage, in 1148. The *Historia pontificalis*, a very well-informed source, tells us—not without humor—how this came about. Ralph used the one effective weapon, money, which he judiciously distributed among the cardinals.[137] Thus, the way was cleared for the comedy acted out at the consistory of Reims. Before it opened, Ralph had sworn—but how valid was the oath of an excommunicated man?—to abide by the papal decision. He appeared at the hearing with his first wife, knowing full well that since mutual consent was henceforth the only consideration, the consistory had to obtain the voluntary compliance of the two persons involved. The outcome thus depended on the abandoned woman and her "party," whose good will had to be won by the promise of an "assuagement" (*consolatio*).[138] In a kindly, paternal manner, Eugenius III himself called upon the first wife to tell her side of the story. Without indicating any desire to return to her husband, she declared her willingness to hear the arguments of the opposing party. At that point, Bishop Bartholomew of Laon, the saintly man who two years later was to retire to the Cistercian monastery of Foigny (note that the Cistercians had "made it," having infiltrated the royal entourage) came forward, ready to swear to the kinship by placing his hand upon the Gospels.[139] The pope cautiously advised him that it would be sufficient if he looked at them from afar. So the oath was received and the divorce pronounced forthwith. Ralph was free to contract a new marriage "in the Lord" (*in domino*). All he had left to do now was to return the dower to his first wife. It turned out that Count Theobald had already received it, and it became clear to everyone that the two families had worked the matter out in advance.

Saint Bernard was present at these dubious solemnities. It was said that he prophesied then and there that nothing good would come of the union that had been regularized by such artifices. In his eyes it remained sullied, for it had been condemned by three successive popes, Innocent, Celestine, and Lucius. And indeed, Ralph soon lost his second wife. He had had three children by her, but the son became a leper and the two daughters remained barren. Clearly, the wrath of God weighed upon this lineage, which became extinct. As for the man who for so long had "scandalized the Church," he was punished in the very place where he had sinned. He took a third wife, but fell ill almost immediately after the wedding. His physician forbade him to make love. He did, anyway, for he was wife-ridden (*uxorius*) like Louis VII, and dominated by his lust. He died three days later, and the county of Vermandois escheated to the count of Flanders by royal favor. The moral of the story was this: The essential wrongdoing of Count Ralph was not adultery, but disobedience; he was "schismatic" and had resisted the Holy See for too long. God punishes those who do not abide by the Church's decisions. The Church was no longer concerned about incest and, provided the proper price was paid, willing to sanction friendly separations if the two families had reached an agreement. Henceforth the Church was glad to stay out of these matters, and the laity was finally free to do as it wished. In 1148, at Reims, Eugenius III used the impediment of kinship to "celebrate a divorce;" a year later at Tusculum he rejected this very argument in order to avoid another divorce which he felt would be dangerous. For him, the essential concern was that his authority be recognized and that "advantage" (*utilitas*), that is, the interests of the Church, be safeguarded. By the middle of the twelfth century the ecclesiastical tribunals were wielding the formidable normative tool that had been forged by Gratian; but since they used it with great flexibility, dispensations were granted more and more frequently. In the final analysis, such a spirit of accommodation allowed the two models of marriage —the lay and the ecclesiastical—to adjust to each other. The knights, and this is what really made the difference, had been won over by the Christian code of morals. More than ever, their preeminence depended on inherited property, and a skilful matrimonial policy was needed to keep that property intact. Canonical impediments of kinship, even those that were inapplicable or had never been applied, were always within reach. They enabled families, if necessary, to circumvent any threats to their policy that might arise from the rigorous positions of the Church. This, then, was the beginning of the age of lawyers, of payoffs, of false witnesses who were paid to swear to spurious genealogies, of all the scandals denounced by Peter the Chanter and his circle of Parisian masters on the eve of the Fourth Lateran Council. John Baldwin has treated this subject so well that there is no need to do it here.[140]

Before leaving this subject, I feel it is necessary to evoke one last affair; and here I can be brief, since these events have been treated in critical studies which, unlike the studies of the other cases, are relevant.[141] I am referring to the divorce of King Philip Augustus. It too concerns the house of Capet and must be seen as a direct prolongation of the other "affairs" I have been considering one by one; to some extent it is a resumé of them all.

Like all his predecessors, Philip Augustus was married young—on 28 April 1180, when he was not quite fifteen years old—though not by his father who, being close to death, was no longer able to act, but by the count of Flanders. Married to a daughter of Ralph of Vermandois who, as we have just seen, was barren, the count arranged the betrothal (*desponsatio*) between the new king and his niece, Elizabeth of Hainaut, a child of nine. In 1184 Philip's kinsmen, his maternal uncles, briefly considered breaking this engagement, which interfered with their own family policy. But in the end the marriage was consummated as soon as the fiancée reached maturity. One son, Louis, was born from this union in 1187. Three years later, however, Elizabeth died without having given another child to the royal house.

Philip left for the Holy Land. Immediately following his return, at the end of 1191, he thought about remarrying. His situation was similar to that of his great-grandfather, Philip I: he had a male heir, but only one, a very young and frail child. The future of the dynasty could indeed be considered precarious, especially since a prophecy circulating at the time predicted that after the end of the seventh generation of Hugh Capet's lineage—that is, after Philip's generation—the crown of France would revert to the descendants of the Carolingians.[142] In keeping with the moral principles enunciated a half-century earlier by the author of the *History of Most Glorious King Louis VII* (*Historia gloriosissimi regis Ludovici VII*)—both those of the family-oriented morality, which called for close attention to the continued existence of the lineage, and those underlying the Church's moral code, which proclaimed that a man of the young king's age and condition must not remain without a legitimate wife—Philip began to search for a consort with as much haste as his father in his own day.

The arrangements were made for his marriage to a king's daughter, Ingeborg of Denmark.

On 15 August 1193, the day after the wedding and on the very day of the solemn coronation of the young couple, the new husband withdrew from his wife for reasons we shall never know. The historian must trust what was said about them by the contemporaries[143] and by the king himself, who spoke of evil charms and impossible carnal union. Ingeborg was repudiated as queens Rosala, Bertha, and Eleanor, and Ralph of Vermandois's first wife had been repudiated. Yet the king was determined to contract another legitimate marriage from which legitimate heirs could be born. He therefore wanted to "celebrate" his divorce and for that purpose seized the usual pretext: the impediment of kinship. On 4 November at Compiègne, before an assembly of prelates and barons presided over by the archbishop of Reims, fifteen swearers—twelve of them members of the royal house—affirmed under oath that the new queen was a cousin in the fourth degree of the late queen. On the grounds of affinity, the union was broken by the country's prelates, just as Louis VII's first marriage was broken at the council of Beaugency. Unlike Eleanor, however, Ingeborg did not accept the decision. Her brother, the king of Denmark, as head of his lineage, took up her cause. Like the count of Champagne who had defended his repudiated niece fifty years earlier, he turned to the pope and the College of Cardinals, declared the degrees of kinship improperly counted—which was obvious—and the oaths specious; moreover, he also produced opposing genealogies. In this awkward situation, Pope Celestine III reacted rather weakly and issued a warning to Philip, who was searching for a new wife. After a number of fruitless attempts, he found her: Agnes, the daughter of the Duke of Méran, became queen in June of 1196. At this juncture, Knut of Denmark increased his pressure on the Roman clergy, demanding anathema for the king of France and interdict for his kingdom. There is no question that the king of France was living in bigamy, like his predecessors Robert and Philip I and like Ralph of Vermandois. Like them, he too came into conflict with papal authority.

This did not happen immediately, not until early 1198, when Innocent III ascended the See of Saint Peter. This pope, conscious of his pastoral responsibilities toward the greatest princes, enjoined Philip to forswear sin and to dismiss his second wife (*superducta*), whose marriage would have to be condemned by the Church in any case because of an impediment on the grounds of affinity, since Agnes's sister was married to the king's nephew. Unlike Philip I and Bertrade, however, Philip Augustus and his wife were never excommunicated, although the mission of the legate Peter of Capua did result in the launching of an interdict against the kingdom in 1200. The pope soon realized that most of the bishops of France refused to carry out the sentence and that it would be dangerous to uphold it in a State that was firmly controlled by its sovereign and where, moreover, heresy was raising its head everywhere. The interdict was therefore quickly lifted. It was sufficient that the king—who had just negotiated the marriage of Prince Louis with the niece of John Lackland—promised under oath not to separate from Ingeborg for seven months, pending a final decision from the Church. This was the essential point: he had to show his submission and to recognize the jurisdictional superiority of the Church of Rome.

The divorce proceedings opened in March 1201 at Soissons, before an assembly of prelates similar to that of Compiègne, in the presence of two new legates. One of these, a kinsman and friend of the king, was notoriously favorable to him, but the other, a Benedictine monk, refused to let himself be bought. Duly surrounded by jurists, the two parties debated, Philip advancing the argument of kinship, the Danes insisting on the obligations incurred. After two weeks of discussions, the king of France suddenly departed with Ingeborg, "escaping the grip of the Romans."[144] In considering the unfolding of this affair, one must not lose sight of the role played by Innocent III's complex diplomacy. At that point, the pope wished to foster an alliance between Philip Augustus and Otto of Brunswick, whom he supported in Germany. This is why he was conciliatory from the outset, and even more so when the second wife (*superducta*) died in August of 1201. In November, the pope agreed to legitimize Agnes's two children—a boy, Philip, who was only a few months old, and a girl—advancing two reasons for this step: On the one hand, the welfare of the kingdom demanded that the king's succession be more secure; on the other hand, Philip was innocent, since, following the decision of Compiègne, he had thought he was free to contract a third marriage. On this last point, the pope actually contradicted himself, for we know that at the beginning of his pontificate he had claimed that the king was disregarding the admonitions of Celestine III. But the most important consideration for Rome was the increase in power that might accrue to it from the ascension to the French throne of a bastard legitimized by a pope.

Nonetheless, the negotiations concerning the divorce continued to drag on for another ten years. Innocent III obstinately refused to reopen the proceedings, well aware of the hold he thus exercised over the Capetian king. Philip kept pressing his case, unquestionably motivated by religious scruples. He was, after all, living in sin, reduced to finding an outlet for his sexual urges in haphazard illegitimate unions. (In 1205 he had a bastard son by a girl belonging to the aristocracy of Arras.) He protested, reminding the pope that the Church had permitted Frederick Barbarossa, most recently John Lackland, and Louis VII to separate from their wives. He kept building up marriage prospects that might be pleasing to the pope in hopes that they would induce him to yield. Throughout this long period the vicissitudes of the papal diplomacy, which was deployed over the entire Western world and had to deal with the problems of the crusade, the Cathar heresy, the troubled situation in Germany, and the wars between the kings of France and England, resulted in alternating phases of strictness and leniency. Nonetheless, the pope and the cardinals, many of whom had ties to the king of France, slowly proceeded toward a solution. Everyone knew that the argument of kinship was worthless: the genealogical investigations pursued within the Capetian house—their findings are preserved in Philip Augustus' registers—had brought to light only one fact, namely, the consanguinity between the king and his first wife.[145] A different argument for annulment therefore gradually took shape—nonconsummation of the marriage. Philip steadfastly claimed that he had not known Ingeborg; but since she obstinately protested to the contrary, it was suggested to the king that he make a distinction between the "mingling of the sexual organs" (*commixio sexuum*), which might have taken place, and the "mingling of seeds in the female vessel" (*commixio seminum in vase muliebri*) which had clearly been impossible. In the end, the king's party was reduced to hoping that the queen might agree to become a nun, a step that would have freed her husband.

In April 1213, as he was preparing to take over England on the suggestion of Innocent III, Philip suddenly announced that he would take back his wife. He was as good as his word, and Ingeborg was henceforth treated as the queen. Yet it cannot be said that he finally bowed to the will of the papacy, which had already made extraordinary concessions. The Church had no reason to celebrate a victory. The fact is that on the eve of embarking on a risky military venture, of a battle for which he needed to feel morally prepared,[146] the king of France meant to cleanse himself of a transgression whose gravity he recognized more clearly now that he was becoming older. It should be added that he was forty-eight years old, that Prince Louis himself had just begotten a son, that Philip, the legitimized son, could take the succession if necessary; in short, that the future of the dynasty was no longer a source of concern.

This last, widely discussed and interminable affair is conclusive in two respects. On the one hand, it marks the end of an era for this exalted lineage: not until the end of the fifteenth century was another king of France to become embroiled in marital difficulties. On the other hand, it is also the end of an era in the history of marriage in the Western world. For it had so clearly demonstrated the discrepancies between matrimonial practices and ecclesiastical theory that it was bound to hasten the papal decision to attenuate officially the Church's exigencies in the matter of incest. For twenty years the case of Philip Augustus occupied the thinking of the theologians, especially Parisian masters like Peter the Chanter, some of whom were directly involved in the bargaining between the pope and the king of France. These men became more forceful in their denunciation of the contradictions caused by the excessive extension of the canonical impediment of kinship. At last, the court of Rome listened to them. In an effort to endow the bond of marriage with greater stability, to limit the occasions for chicanery, and to make the procedures for granting dispensations more credible, the Lateran Council espoused the propositions of these masters in 1215[147] and reduced the incest prohibition from the seventh to the fourth degree of kin-ship. This decision was the final consecration of a conciliation—which *de facto* had been in preparation for more than a century—between the ecclesiastical theory of marriage and the practices traditionally followed by the lay aristocracy.

III.

A Noble House:
The Counts of Guines

Having pointed out that by the middle of the twelfth century a certain adjustment between the priestly injunctions and the matrimonial practices of the laity was under way, I shall now consider this conciliation from a different angle, and on the basis of a different set of writings. These texts too were composed by clerics, but clerics in the service of temporal lords, and these men described what their masters were doing or what they would like to do. At the time and in the region under study here, such writings were rare. There is no use looking for them in the archives, although one might occasionally find a few documents, especially acts pertaining to the clauses of the betrothal gift (*sponsalicium*), that have by chance been preserved in the depth of ecclesiastical collections, but almost all of these date from before the first third of the eleventh century. And while it is true that in the southern provinces of Europe, in Latium or at Genoa,[1] certain notarial records reveal that in the course of the twelfth century very gradual changes in the respective rights of the spouses were made in order to adjust the juridical practices to the underlying assumptions of society, no such observation is possible for northern France. Here archival documents can further an investigation in only one way, i.e., by enabling historians—and this is already a greal deal—to reconstitute certain aristocratic genealogies and to discern the influence of matrimonial practices on the destiny of a given lineage. Somewhat richer information is provided by certain narratives, both the fictitious accounts of the literature of amusement—which I urge social historians to re-read very carefully—and the somewhat less fictional accounts composed to glorify a house. The latter concern only families of the very highest nobility; at least they project the image that was considered appropriate to such status. We can learn a great deal about this image—as well as about other traits of aristocratic mentality, which I shall discuss in another context[2]—from works of this kind, as you will see when I show you one extremely rich example, the *History of the Counts of Guines* (*Historia comitum Ghisnensium*), written between 1201 and 1206.[3]

This work is an outstanding testimony to the development of a genealogical literature which by the second half of the twelfth century had become authentic history, for it is a series of biographies serving as the focal points of a family's memories.[4] The *History* describes the past of two lineages, that of the counts of Guines and that of the seigneurs of Ardres, which had just become allied through a marriage.[5] The author, Lambert, was a cleric and served in the household of Ardres.He was a priest, married, and father of at least one daughter and two sons, both of whom were also priests (*sacerdotes*)—another precise piece of information that permits us to measure the distance between actual behavior and a theoretical moral code. Lambert took great pride in being a "master," like the other masters whom Count Baldwin of Guines lodged in his household, where they translated for their patron— himself "unlettered" (*illiteratus*)—the most important books of the ecclesiastical libraries, notably two works, the *Song of Songs* and the writings of Saint Augustine, that served as reference works for the theologians of marriage. Lambert's work, then, partook of both the learned and the profane culture. Composed in Latin, it is filled with reminiscences of the poets, and the rules of rhetoric inform every one of its sentences. Yet this writer was also well acquainted with the most recent trends of the vernacular literature of amusement[6] and certainly treated his family history from a very laicized perspective. He endeavored to give an account of the family's origin three centuries earlier. His only solid support, however, was provided by the memory of the house, which did not go back beyond the middle of the eleventh century. For the earlier periods, Lambert used his imagination and transposed into the most remote past the attitudes held by the seigneurs of his own time. But such anachronisms are most valuable for our purposes, because they uncover a whole vision of the world and tell us what people living at a small princely court of northern France were thinking around the year 1200, at the time of the divorce of Philip Augustus and of such men as Peter the Chanter, Robert de Courson, and Stephen Langton.

Marriage occupies a central position in Lambert's account. First and foremost, it serves as the controlling principle of the discourse. Faced with the task of describing the destinies of two separate lineages, starting with their respective founding ancestors and even including a number of adventitious branches, since some of these became allied by marriage with one or the other of the main branches, Lambert follows the thread of a succession of "generations."[7] Throughout the *History*, beginning with the unions concluded by the mythical ancestors, Lambert's account is thus held together by a succession of legitimate and fruitful unions. The links of this double chain of heirs are bound together by a succession of wives.

Even more illustrative, it seems to me, of the importance of the marriage pact in aristocratic society—and probably in society as a whole—is the manner in which social space was organized within the house (*domus*). A famous passage in Lambert's *History*[8] describes the dwelling built by Arnulf II of Ardres in the first third of the twelfth century. The house itself was still but a wooden structure, but marvelous in its interior arrangements: "It would be impossible to count all the doors and windows". . ."of this inextricable labyrinth (*inextricabile laberintum*)." The reason for Lambert's delight was a new differentiation of the domestic space. The house, he tells us, was built on three levels; on the middle level, designed to accommodate the living quarters (*habitatio*) and all communal activities (*conversatio*), was one room, set apart from the communal quarters yet placed at the very core of the entire design. This was "the great bedchamber of the lord and his wife, where they sleep." It not only had access to the dormitory of the small children (*pueri*) and the servant-girls and to the warming-room, a veritable incubator for the suckling infants, but also was connected with the third level, housing the two rooms where, on one side the adolescent boys slept "when they wanted to" and on the other the adolescent girls "because it was proper that they should." Clearly, then, the house was conceived for one couple, one manifest physical union. There was only one bedchamber, only one bed, the forge or *fabrica*—recall the meaning of that word in the work of Bernard Sylvester—where the future of the lineage was "founded" in the dark of night. As for the many other persons included in the household, whether they were kinsfolk—uncles, aunts, brothers, or unmarried sisters—, visiting friends, or the domestic servants, they lived a gregarious existence wherever there was room in the other parts of the building. The house (*domus*) was a "birthing-place," and its physical structure revealed the true nature of the household: It was a two–generation family.

Marriage also occupied a central position in the rituals of society, another fact that is strikingly illustrated by the *History*. It is true that the few chronological landmarks that had become fixed in the family's memory did not concern marriage, but burial (for here the dates were permanently committed to memory by epitaphs and obituaries), and that in the case of the real hero of the account, Arnulf IV of Ardres, eldest son and heir of Count Baldwin II of Guines, the only precise date given is his knighting.[9] But then the family's marriages are always discussed in great detail and form the very core of the multiple biographies that constitute this gallery of ancestors. The solemn proceedings are always presented—as was indeed proper—in two phases. First comes the betrothal (*desponsatio*). Here Lambert, attesting to the effects of the Church's exhortations on the moral code of the laity, goes out of his way to prove the consent (*consensus*) of the prospective spouses, especially that of the girls. Here, for instance, is his account of the occasion taking place sometime between 1148 and 1150 when Baldwin, the present count, "married" the only daughter—and hence heiress—of the only surviving sister—and hence heiress—of the seigneur of Ardres, who had died childless. (The agreement was concluded when Baldwin was extremely young, for we know that the ceremony of his knighting, performed by Thomas Becket, took place only ten years later.) In any case, Lambert tells us that when the bride was brought before the large audience assembled in her father's house, "she expressed her willingness by the happy expression of her face," which was sufficient to satisfy the two contracting parties and to give the signal for the unanimous acclamation needed to seal the pact.[10] All this took place many years before the wedding. Following that ceremony the young couple, having reached maturity at last, took up residence in the house of Ardres, the bride's house, since she was an heiress. This house was at their disposal because the bride's mother was living in the house of her second husband, the viscount of Merck, while Baldwin's father still occupied the house of Guines. It was in the bride's house, then, in the great chamber (*magna camera*) I have just described, and in the bed that was awaiting them, that the young couple hastened to conceive and give birth to five living children before 1169 (the date when Baldwin became the count of Guines upon the death of his father and transferred his bed to the castle of Guines) and five more children thereafter, until the mother, totally exhausted, died in childbirth.

Concerning the marriage rituals (*nuptiae*), Lambert also provides outstanding testimony.[11] In 1194 Arnulf, the eldest son of the marriage I have just described, had been searching for a wife for some time. We know that, by contrast to his father, he had been knighted for thirteen years; but then the house had gained in power between his father's generation and his own, so that a good match was more difficult to make. In the end, however, Arnulf too found an heiress, that of the lords of the neighboring castle of Bourbourg. Immediately following the death of this girl's only brother, he had pounced upon her, although this involved breaking the faith (*fides*) he had earlier promised to a daughter of the count of Saint-Pol. (On this point, the lay practices were less concerned about the ecclesiastical code of morals; the act of breaking the betrothal [*sponsalia*] seems to have been a very simple matter.) Arnulf's father asked and obtained the necessary dispensations first from the bishop of Thérouanne and then from the archbishop of Reims, for the lady whose expectations Arnulf coveted was his cousin in the fourth degree. The way was cleared for the ceremony by which the eldest son of the count of Guines took to himself a lawful wife and was united in marriage (*legitimam uxorem sibi adjunxit et copulavit matrimonio*). The first step was the betrothal (*desponsatio*), by which the spouses exchanged their mutual consent and the bride was handed over in exchange for a dower, consisting of the seigneury of Ardres and one of its annexes. The solemn wedding took place soon thereafter. The Church was asked, of course, to celebrate it, and Lambert himself, as the resident priest of Ardres, was called upon to ring the bells. Out of excessive zeal, he refused. For Arnulf was under excommunication for having torn down a widow's mill (note that the Church's old provisions for the protection of those who were left defenseless by the destruction of the conjugal cell were still enforced), and word that the *officialis* of Reims had recently absolved the young bridegroom had not yet reached Ardres. Lambert tells us that it was precisely in order to appease Count Baldwin, who had been very angry at his refusal to participate in the wedding ceremonies, that he started to write his work. Having reached this point in his narrative, he describes the ceremony itself.

Significantly, everything he tells us about it takes place at night. As soon as the new husband and wife

have bedded down together, Lambert, his two sons—
who, it will be recalled, were also priests—and the
priest of another parish in the castellany of Ardres
come in to sprinkle the couple with holy water. They
also circle the bed in order to cense it from all sides,
bless the newlyweds and commit them to God's keeping.[12] Thereupon, and it is this last ritual that is
emphasized, it is the father of the groom, not of the
bride—in other words, the *caput generis* and head of the
house whose future is at stake—who preempts the
officiating function in the celebration of a cultic ritual
of generation. Lifting his hands and eyes toward
heaven and adapting a formula taken from the Acts of
the Apostle Thomas by the ecclesiastical ritual in this
region, he beseeches God to bless his children, "joined
together by a holy copulation and by the rites of marriage"—thereby endorsing, incidentally, the Church's
contention that the conjugal union is complete before
the sexual union (*commixio sexus*)—so that they will
remain steadfast in harmony and that "their seed will
be multiplied in the length of days and throughout all
ages." Having thus besought God's blessing, he be-
stows his own blessing on the couple, thereby adding a
kind of familial consecration to the consecration that
has already taken place. By his gestures and his words
he passes on to the new couple on whom henceforth
the future of the family depends the hereditary charis-
ma vested in him, the father. By the end of the twelfth
century, the Church had gained a firm hold over the
wedding ceremony. Nonetheless, the wedding itself remained essentially a domestic rite designed to promote
fertility, a prelude to the deflowering of the bride who,

it was ardently hoped, would immediately conceive. All the worldly aspects of the wedding ceremony were engulfed in the festivities that started the next morning, three days of games and feasting[13] designed to impress the minds of the crowd of invited guests with the memory of a great social event.

Lastly, Lambert's account also reveals the central position of marriage within the moral code of the laity. The purpose of marriage was procreation, the planting of seed in the woman's womb, the legitimate—and abundant—act of impregnation. What more proof of this is needed than the rhythm of births and the number of legitimate children who survived the mortal perils of infancy in each of the fertile unions of all the lineages described by Lambert? Yet the sexual activity of the males was not imprisoned within the confines of marriage. Men were proud of their sexual exploits, which are treated as a matter of course in the account I am using here—a laudatory account, mind you, that meant to preach by example and to pass on a set of moral values to future generations. Our author therefore constantly dwells on the purity of all the daughters of the family and all the wives whom it has received. Whenever he speaks at any length of a mother or a grandmother, he is sure to tell us that she came into her master's bed as a virgin. In the household, the virgin daughters of the family were watched much more carefully, it would appear, than the maidens whom we encounter in the heroes' successful nocturnal adventures in the courtly romances. At the castle of Ardres, the young girls were prudently led to their communal bedchamber on the highest and least accessible floor. But even this refuge was not always considered safe enough, so that a nunnery (*claustrùm sanctimonalium*)[14] was frequently built next to the dwelling for the express purpose of protecting the widows of the house, as well as any girls too misshapen to marry, from pollution of any kind. The same cloister, however, also served to shield those daughters whom the family did hope to cede some day to its best advantage and whose value therefore had to be kept intact.

By contrast, the sexual prowess of men is loudly acclaimed. Let us look at the most flattering portrait of this gallery of ancestors, that of Count Baldwin II, the very man for whom the book was written. In chapter 88, entitled "Concerning prudence and negligence" (*De prudentia et de negligentia*), Lambert speaks of his virtues and of his shortcomings—and we can be sure that these were the shortcomings the count wished to be talked about. "From the beginning of adolescence until his old age, his loins were stirred by the intemperance of an impatient libido"; to be precise, "very young girls, and especially virgins, aroused his desire"; and in his exploits he surpassed David, Solomon, and even Jupiter.[15] Surely, this is high praise. Lambert adds that these amusements did not remain unfruitful, mentioning along the way five bastard sons, two of whom were canons; although, as Lambert says, Baldwin by no means knew them all. But we now do know, from the chronicle written between 1226 and 1234 at the monastery of Andres, the foundation and burial place of the counts of Guines, that the funeral of Count Baldwin II in 1206 was attended by thirty-three of his sons and daughters "who had come either from his wife or from elsewhere."[16] The count had begotten ten living legitimate children; consequently, he was survived by at least twenty-three bastards of both sexes, who mourned him along with the members of the legitimate family.

The genetic vigor of the males was thus widely disseminated beyond the lineal descent group, but toward whom? The women who were enjoyed by men of great family along the way are always called "beautiful" and frequently "noble" by Lambert.[17] As for the servant girls and the prostitutes who might briefly distract them, these men preferred that nothing be said about them. The partners whom they did acknowledge may have been the daughters of their vassals, but there is more evidence that they were the family's bastard daughters, who formed a kind of pleasure reserve within the house itself. Illegitimate sexuality thus appears to have been of a strongly endogamous nature. Here, for instance, are two young men, the sons of a lord of Ardres and of a mother who, by Lambert's time, was said to have "brought bad blood" into the family.[18] The first of these young men had to wait for his marriage—for the bed of the house was not vacant—until the death of his father, who is known to have had four bastard sons, good knights all of them. While he thus had to exercise patience, he begot two sons of two different mothers (and one of these sons eventually obtained for one of *his* sons the hand of the daughter of the priest Lambert, who was very proud of this honorable union). Baldwin, the brother of the young man above, had a first bastard son by the daughter—and we are expressly told that she was "virgin"—of a canon, Ralph, himself the bastard son of Baldwin's grandfather, and consequently his uncle. (This, incidentally, provides some additional information about the function of the canons' chapter which, a counterpart to the girls' convent, was adjoined to the house [*domus*] and gave shelter to the boys of the family, legitimate or not, but was certainly no citadel of chastity.) Baldwin subsequently had two children by another noble girl whom he also deflowered. Her father was another canon and her mother, his legitimate wife, was "a noble lady." The fact that Baldwin had two children by this girl indicates that this was a case of prolonged concubinage, which is rare, since bastards were usually scattered far and wide. In addition, Baldwin had a son who became a knight and a daughter who was most renowned (*famosissima*) for having slept first with a brother of Baldwin II of Guines and then with a canon, this one of the cathedral chapter of Thérouanne. All of this was perfectly open. The offspring of these wayward unions rightfully belonged to the house,[19] and Baldwin II is specifically commended for having provided his bastard sons with good training, either in the military or in the Church, and for having arranged, just like King Henry I of England, very good marriages for his bastard daughters.[20]

Yet it should be noted that this venereal pleasure (*delectatio Veneris*), of which the males of these families were so proud, was only given free rein either before marriage, during their "youth" and in the prolonged state of celibacy that was the lot of most of the canons, or after marriage, when the head of the family had become widowed, as in the case of Baldwin II. Throughout a man's married life, such dissolute behavior may have occurred, but we do not hear about it, for it was not considered seemly to mention it. It seems to me that this pattern of behavior is extremely significant; as significant, indeed, as the praise given to conjugal love in this account. Lambert goes to considerable length to dramatize the lament at the loss of Count Baldwin's wife. The count, he tells us, was in England. Word came that his wife's delivery, the tenth at least, was expected to be difficult. He hurried back. By the time he arrived, the physicians had given up all hope and left him alone with the parturient woman, so that he might "console" her. When she died, he fell ill. He, who was normally seen on horseback, full of vigor, lay down and bolted his door "for days on end."[21] Quite clearly, the elder (*senior*) made a point of cherishing his lady and of cherishing his children.[22] The ethos of the eldest son, the head of the house, was constructed around one main axis: he must reserve his seed for the one woman who had been conveyed to his bed in a solemn wedding procession; and he must raise his eldest son to be a good knight and give him a good wife.

In essence, then, the obligation of the head of the family (*caput generis*) was the careful husbanding of the seed contained in his loins and in those of his legitimate sons. It was a duty that was not always easy to fulfill and could become the source of grave concern.

Count Manasses of Guines, Baldwin II's great-uncle, saw his hair turn white with anxiety: His only daughter had died, and his only granddaughter was sickly. "He was very much afraid that if no seed issued from his own body were to survive, he would have to beg an heir for the domain of Guines from one of his sisters (all his brothers had died without heirs) "as if from another man's seed" (*"quasi ab alio semine"*).[23] At least he was free to arrange the marriage of that granddaughter as he saw fit, in consultation with his wife, who did indeed speak up. The girl's father had nothing to say in the matter; after he had become widowed, he had remarried and therefore no longer held any rights to his first wife's inheritance. For any decision concerning the family's marriages belonged to those who were responsible for the destiny of the patrimony, to the males of the lineage; above all, to the man who acted as their head.[24] And if the patrimony was a fief, the decision also belonged to him who was the seigneur of the fief.[25]

The interference of the feudal seigneur in the marriage strategies of other lineages was a new phenomenon when Lambert wrote his work;[26] but here too he enlightens us. First of all, it is significant that he includes the accomplishment of this duty in his portrait of the exemplary seigneur. Baldwin, who had become a better man through his wife's death—although this did not prevent him from chasing after little virgins—now practiced the royal virtues, setting himself up as the devoted comforter of orphans, the helpful defender of widows. His special solicitude was for noble orphans who had been despoiled by their kinsmen, for it could happen that the youths (*juvenes*) wrought vengeance for their frustrations upon the minor children temporarily entrusted to their discretion by the death of the head of the house. To such orphans Baldwin would give wives capable of "exalting" them by bringing them wealth and honor.[27] In other words, it was he who gave in marriage. To be sure, in this case the beneficiaries of his efforts were orphans, and one wonders whether he would have substituted for a living father in this manner. However that may be, he showed his largesse to the world, which saw him in the role of wife-giver.[28] He could only play this role because a number of women were his to give away, chiefly his bastard daughters (and the fact that they could serve this worthy cause was a good excuse for him to beget as many of them as possible), but also, no doubt, the widows and daughters of deceased vassals.

In any case, the involvement of the feudal seigneur in the arrangement of marriages was considered perfectly normal and customary by the time our text was written, as we can clearly see from one of the episodes of the *History*. Here the author obviously transposes the practices of his own day into an era of the past beyond reliable memory, where he is free to deploy his imagination. At the mythical origin of the lineage of the seigneurs of Ardres he places a woman, just as he places a young man at the equally mythical origin of the lineage of the counts of Guines. Male and female (symbolically expressing the subordination of castle to county), this pair of founding ancestors appears as a kind of guiding prefiguration of that best hope of the dynasty, the new couple united by the marriage of 1194. The mythical ancestress is a virgin, an orphan, alone, desolate and destitute (*sola, desolata, destituta*)— very much like the orphans who benefit from the solicitude of exemplary seigneurs. She is at odds with the count of Guines, her "cousin," who is also the overlord of her land, and who intends to give her a husband she does not want. In order to escape the pressure of this elder (*senior*), she converts her allod into a fief held from her uncle, the bishop of Thérouanne. This was a common procedure in 1200, but certainly not in the remote past, about which Lambert can only dream. Thereupon this uncle arranges her marriage, finding her a "good knight," a man "equal to the task of protecting the land," and then, after the death of the first, gives her a second, equally capable husband.

Lambert amply describes the behavior of all these men who were empowered to make decisions concerning marriages either by their position within the physical family or by their position within the fictitious family created by the feudal bond. Their duty was to make the best possible use of the exchange value of their daughters, whose chief virtue was to submit to their choice.[29] They had, after all, been brought into the world precisely because they could be transplanted, like the tender cuttings the skillful vinedresser nurses to fruition, into fertile ground where they could bring forth the illustrious offspring who in turn would become attached to the family trunk by the feelings of special affection they owed their maternal uncles.[30] All those who had daughters to give in marriage hoped to distribute all of them outside their own house. Some were able to do this; the viscount of Merck, for example, who married off his nine daughters, or Baldwin II who married off and even arranged remarriages for his four legitimate daughters.[31]

But everyone was not so successful. Arnulf II of Guines was left with two of his eight daughters on his hands, Henry of Bourbourg with three of his five.[32] These young women were pledged, as a meager spiritual compensation, to the life of virginal perfection for which the family convent was designed. Such failures can be explained, of course, as the reverse side of the marriage strategies pursued by this society, as the result of the constraints that limited the chances of marriage for boys. For it was felt that the structure of the family and the necessity of entrusting only one couple in each house with the task of procreation called for great prudence. And this necessity was compelling. Henry of Bourbourg had seven sons by his second wife. The eldest of these had been married twice, but without success; he died without offspring. Two sons were placed in the Church. Of the four others, two died "young"—that is, unmarried—killed in one of the frequent accidents of chivalric sport, in which a third son lost an eye, so that he was ineligible to assume the honor of his father. At this point, the family hastened to arrange a marriage for the youngest son, born after the death of the eldest, whose name he bore. In cavalier disregard of impediments on the grounds of affinity, he was married to his sister-in-law's sister, for it was vital to preserve a beneficial alliance with the house of Béthune. A man as amply provided with male offspring as Henry of Bourbourg thus found himself with only one grandson, a sickly boy who died young, and one granddaughter, who became the heiress of the patrimony[33]—and she was the young girl whom the son of the count of Guines was, for that very reason, so anxious to marry in 1194.

This story reveals the risks inherent in the prudent strategy of the elders (*seniores*). In principle, it certainly did benefit the lineage, for it meant that the supply of potential brides was very large and that noble families could choose the very best—descendants of Charlemagne, of whom there were quite a few in this region, the sisters or nieces of princes, and also those women who, in the absence of male claimants capable of contesting their right to the succession, would bring the entire fortune of their house into the marriage. In order to capture such a prize, the husband was willing to "humiliate" himself and to take as his wife, "following the example of many noblemen, dukes, kings, and emperors, the daughter of one of his men."[34] Whenever they could promise the advantage of such a succession, the givers of wives had the upper hand in the bargaining, and the inequality between the spouses became reversed. The heads of such houses set out to find the best possible match for the heiresses that were theirs to bestow and did not hesitate to break a first marriage if the expectations of the young woman had increased.[35] And indeed, such rich prizes were usually reaped by young men of the very highest rank, scions of powerful houses who, for that reason, won out in the competition. In fact, the number of such heiresses was surprisingly high: in the span of just a half-century, between 1150 and 1200, the patrimony of the counts of Guines, that of the castellans of Bourbourg, and, on two occasions, that of the seigneurs of Ardres thus fell to females and hence came under the control of a son-in-law. The concerted effort of families to deprive most of their sons of legitimate procreation was bound to weaken the dynasty. And yet our text shows just as clearly that this policy attained its main objective, for it did preserve the wealth of the house. In the course of these two centuries covered by Lambert's account, none of the main trunks of these lineages permitted the sprouting of sidebranches, that is, the division of inheritances. At every generation, one male only took over the entire patrimony. This was made possible by the elimination of his brothers, who were shunted toward the clergy or a monastery, toward adventures in the Holy Land or in England, or toward the deadly hazards of military apprenticeship and practice. Like the aristocracy of the region of Mâcon, this aristocracy appears as a very stable group. Indeed, it was probably too stable for its own good, for while we do not see the founding of any new houses, we do see the extinction of existing ones. In the final analysis, this marriage strategy tended to promote the progressive concentration of aristocratic fortunes.

Yet there are indications that this behavior was beginning to change during the second half of the twelfth century. Consider the case of Arnulf IV of Guines. He had five brothers, one of whom became a cleric, and one of whom was killed "in the flower of youth" (*in flore juventutis*). But the three others married and each became the head of a house, complete with a dwelling located within a small seigneury. This land was part of the family's holdings that the father had set aside for this purpose; it was not taken, to be sure, from the core of the ancestral domain, but from lands recently acquired either by clearing or by purchase.[36] Here I see a clearer example of a phenomenon I had earlier noticed in the region of Mâcon, although for a somewhat later period. It is a phenomenon that is corroborated by the archeology of the noble dwelling, which from that time onward shows increased evidence of new constructions, satellites of the old castles, that were soon to be called fortified houses (*maisons-fortes*). No doubt such a reversal of family policy was facilitated by the increased wealth of the lineages. After 1150, the cultivation of landed properties became more intensive, the fiscal powers of all noble seigneurs brought in more and more cash, and the fiscal powers of the great princes began to provide them with the means to distribute handsome pensions among the nobility. Under these conditions, the head of a family (*caput generis*) no longer needed to be quite so parsimonious. Moreover, I believe that marriage for younger sons was facilitated by a new development in legal practices, namely, the increasing use of the feudal contract to maintain the unity of a patrimony that was broken up in order to provide for the establishment of sons other than the eldest. Here again, Lambert projects the ideal image of a usage that was current when he wrote into the remote past of which he dreamt. He speaks about an imaginary count of Ponthieu who divided his inheritance among four sons at the beginning of the tenth century. The eldest received the ancestral house, that is, Ponthieu; the next two were given important portions, the counties of Boulogne and Saint-Pol, but only as fiefs; and the fourth was promised the county of Guines. As it happened, some remote descendants of the first owner of this honor had just reclaimed this property, so that the count of Ponthieu was obliged to provide for the establishment of this last son by finding an heiress for him, in this case, the heiress of the count of Saint-Valéry.[37] The count of Ponthieu, a mythical hero, and yet the spokesman for the dominant ideology of his author's time, thus uses the tool of feudal subordination to create a tight bond between the central core of the dynasty's domain and the dissociated parts of the patrimony, that is, the new houses where the various younger sons are living; which was exactly what Count Baldwin II was doing in the concrete reality of the late twelfth century. By marrying his younger sons to the daughters of his vassals, Baldwin also made them his vassals; in due course they would even become vassals of their oldest brother. In any case, it seems to me that this change in attitude toward the marriage of boys had the most far-reaching consequences. It was part of a more general change within the nobility as a whole. Other indications of change at that time are furnished by the breakdown of castellanies, the contraction of the banal seigneury within the parish limits, and the reduction of differences between princes and knights.

In principle, then, the matrimonial arrangements I have described here were initiated by the head of the house. It should be noted, however—and this will be my last observation—that Lambert's writing pursues a clearly visible intent. He does his best not to make too much of the decisive authority of the elders (*seniores*) —which he does exalt in the passages devoted to their praise—by celebrating another, contradictory accomplishment, the personal role the *juvenes* were supposedly playing in the pursuit of an excellent match. His entire account, after all, is centered upon the figure of a young husband, and thus bound to include the praise of youth. And youth was by nature predatory. It gloried, not only in the casual deflowering of virgins but also in seducing (*se ducere*) the lady destined to become the young man's good wife and the mother of the future seigneur. In the process of devoting a great deal of space to the praise of "youth," Lambert's *History* comes to a positive appraisal of the act of abduction, which was condemned as an offense by the moral code of the heads of houses (*capita mansorum*), but placed among the foremost acts of valor in the moral code of the bachelors. But in a society that was becoming less brutal each day, the proprieties demanded that abduction be given a more sophisticated and sublimated form. It would not do for a young knight to take a noble woman by force; he had to win her favor by showing off his personal valor and the glory he had acquired in tournaments and in the other combats involved in the games of courtly love. We should see the tournament —which was indeed an entertainment that had its heyday during this period and played a considerable role in the history of the counts of Guines—as a kind of exhibition, where eligible bachelors preened themselves under the eyes of the ladies, but especially under the eyes of those who had a woman to bestow. All the heroes of this family chronicle are shown as excellent jousters during their youth; and if, to give one example, Arnulf, the second seigneur of Ardres of that name—a young man who was free to choose his own wife, since his father was dead and he had no uncle—was able to obtain a wife from the glorious house of Alost, it was, Lambert tells us, because the fame of his athletic reputation had won over the chief of that lineage, who gave him his sister.[38] But the principal means of deploying the ideology of youth in the *History* is the description of the posturing of courtly love. This description appears twice, and in two crucial sections of the work. It is no coincidence—for the fascination with the values of youth demanded that they be celebrated with great *éclat*—that at both ends of the long chain formed by the lineage of the counts of Guines the author places a young man, both seducers.

The founding myth is embodied in an imaginary hero, a Viking, though garbed as a young court fop of 1200. The son of a king, embarked upon youthful adventures, but also the legitimate heir of the earliest counts of Guines, we see him "retained" in the house of the count of Flanders, where he is a member of the band led by the master's eldest son. All of this takes place in the early years of the tenth century, but this does not prevent Lambert from showing us the adventurer as a knighted warrior and vassal of the patron who receives him. In this household, he outshines all his companions by his virtues, wins the heart of the count's "very beautiful" sister and, "in playing the game," ends up making her pregnant. In other words, he uses her as it would be normal for any young knight to use the bastard daughters of the family or the daughters of vassals. But never the sister of one's lord, for this was felony. The seducer, therefore, having scored his point, hastily retreats to Guines, where he pines away "like another Andrew (the Chaplain)."[39] Nonetheless, the fruit of this guilty union, a boy, is brought up by his cousin, who acts as his godfather, sponsors his knighting, and eventually establishes him—and here we see the emergence of a more positive attitude toward bastardhood—as the founder of a new line of counts of Guines.

When speaking of the remote descendant of this legitimized bastard, Arnulf "the younger," Lambert no longer dreams, but reports what he has seen and what is a source of pride in the house where he serves. Immediately upon Arnulf's knighting, Count Baldwin organized every detail of a long and costly tour from tournament to tournament in order to show off his eldest son. This would enhance his glory and impress those who were casting about for marriage prospects for their daughters with a dazzling display of personal renown in addition to the family's renown.

After at least five years of such wandering, "the hero and the glory of the house of Guines" at last became so famous that he attracted the attention of Countess Ida of Boulogne. Now this woman, who had just become widowed for the second time, was a fabulous prize, offering Carolingean blood and immense properties to the man who would take her. Moreover, she enjoyed the game of love. Ida fell in love with Arnulf or, "in her feminine fickleness and wiliness," pretended to love him. Arnulf, for his part, fell in love with Ida or, "in his masculine sagacity and cunning," pretended to love her; "for in seeking the favors of the countess by this true or pretended love, he aspired to the land and the dignity of the county of Boulogne."[40] It would be impossible to speak more plainly. Lambert, as I pointed out earlier, made use of everything he had learned from the new literature of amusement; but what he tells us about love in his realistic account identifies the conduct of love as a social ritual much more clearly than the testimony of the poets. Lambert demystifies courtly love and shows it for what it was—fundamentally mysogenous. Woman was an object and, as such, contemptible; and the words used to characterize the conduct of Ida—who actually was a deceitful person—are explicit indeed.[41]

An exaltation of gaiety, the game, and pleasure, and a summons to break the threefold injunction against abduction, adultery, and fornication, courtly love does assume the appearance of a threefold defiance of the power of those who arrange marriages, the exhortations of the Church, and a moral code centered upon marriage. But this defiance is only apparent. Ultimately, the whole game was directed by the heads of houses, by Baldwin standing behind Arnulf and Philip of Alsace standing behind Ida. Ultimately, the Church too was fighting to give free rein to affection (*dilectio*) and showed the greatest indulgence for extramarital sexuality.[42] And finally, we can observe even here— some years before Guilleaume de Lorris undertook to recount the seduction of a maiden in the first *Roman de la Rose*—that the games of love were deployed as part of a whole series of maneuvers, all of them leading up to marriage, and that all the posturing ultimately served only as a cover for the ruthless pursuit of a policy strictly designed to further the interests of the lineage.

In the final analysis, Lambert of Ardres's work reveals the ambiguity of the aristocratic ideology with respect to marriage. This ambiguity was fueled by the new orientation of marriage strategies that made it possible for many more sons of aristocratic families to take a legitimate wife. At the same time, this ambiguity increasingly tended to converge with the first adjustments made in the ecclesiastical model of marriage after 1160, under the pontificate of Alexander III.[43] In this region, on the eve of Bouvines, a variety of changes, all of which testify to the emergence of more flexible social relations at the threshold of that glorious thirteenth century, finally brought a reconciliation. Henceforth, there was no unbridgeable gap between the attitudes of the clergy and those of the "great" with respect to the institution of marriage. And even within the thinking of all members of a knighthood that had by then thoroughly absorbed the tenets of Christian morality, a reconciliation had taken place between two models of behavior, that of the bachelors and that of the married men (*conjugati*). Since henceforth most young men eventually did marry, the celibate and the married state no longer characterized two separate and fundamentally hostile groups within high society; for these two states now normally succeeded each other in the course of a man's life. In the final analysis, they complemented each other. In this manner, the nobleman's ethos combined the values appropriate to both these stages of life. On the one hand, it valued the strength of youth (*virtus juventutis*) that projected its energy outward and beyond the house (*domus*), and yet served it by pursuing a wide-ranging quest, from which the young man would bring back both "glory" (that is to say profit, the gifts of princes, and the wages that would augment the resources of the patrimony) and the right wife. On the other hand, it valued the sagacity of the elders (*prudentia seniorum*), the inward-looking, domestic virtue that was the wellspring of the solicitude on behalf of the property which necessarily involved both the wife and her husband, united, as Hugh of Saint-Victor would have it, "in a unique and special way by the love they share."[44]

Notes

Foreword

1. *Speculum* 35 (1960): 1–16, reprinted in Fred A. Cazel, Jr., ed., *Feudalism and Liberty: Articles and Addresses of Sidney Painter* (Baltimore, 1961), pp. 195–219.
2. (Paris, 1973).
3. *Western Attitudes towards Death from the Middle Ages to the Present* (Baltimore, 1974).

Chapter I

1. Georges Duby, Introductory Lecture at the XXIV Settimana Internazionale di Studio, Spoleto, 1976: "Il

matrimonio nella società altomedievale" (proceedings to be published).

2. Burchard of Worms, *Decretorum libri viginti,* in J.-P. Migne, ed., *Patrologiae cursus completus . . . series latina* (Paris, 1844–1903) [hereafter *PL*] 140, 947.

3. Dhuoda, *Manuel pour mon fils,* bk. 8, ch. 14, P. Riché, ed., *Sources chrétiennes* (Paris, 1975), 225: 318: "ora pro parentibus genitoris tui qui illi res suas in legitima dimiserunt hereditate." The kin-group is enumerated in the *Manuel* (bk. 10, ch. 5, Riché, ed., p. 354): The grandfather, the grandmother, and the uncles and aunts on the maternal side form the *domus* in the world of the dead. It consists of two generations, whose head is Dhuoda's father-in-law.

4. J. B. Molin and P. Mutembé, *Le rituel du mariage en France du XIIe au XVIe siècle* (Paris, 1974). See p. 159 for the ritual, of English origin, that was in use at Laon at the beginning of the twelfth century.

5. Cf. the remarks of J. Cuisenier concerning the present-day Islamic world in *Economie et parenté, leur affinité de structure dans le domaine turc et le domaine arabe* (Paris and The Hague, 1975), especially p. 456. Among the many useful studies of marriage by anthropologists, special attention should be given to C. Meillassoux, *Femmes, greniers, et capitaux* (Paris, 1975).

6. Gilbert of Limerick, *Liber de statu ecclesie, PL* 159, 997. "I do not say that it is the function of women to pray, work the land, and fight; they are married to those who pray, work the land, and fight; and they serve them."

7. This idea is already found in the oaths of peace sworn by the knights in 1025. Cf. the decree of Garin of Beauvais, published by R. Bonnaud-Delamare, "Les institutions de paix dans la province ecclésiastique de Reims," in Comité des travaux historiques, ed., *Bulletin philologique et historique, 1955–56* (1957).

8. In this system of values, note the respective shortcomings of the two sexes (which are also their virtues; an

ambivalence that arises from the inversion of the individual's conduct depending on whether it takes place inside or outside of marriage): the "charm" of the bewitching female and the "violence" of the predatory male. On abduction as the exploit of young men, see Jacques Rossiaud, "Prostitution, jeunesse, et société dans les villes du Sud-Est au XVe siècle," *Annales, E.S.C.* 31 (March–April 1976): 289–325. English translation in Robert Forster and Orest Ranum, eds., *Deviants and the Abandoned in French Society* (Baltimore, 1978).

9. On the evolution of the chivalric ideal in the twelfth century, see the recent work of J. Flori, in particular, "La notion de chevalerie dans les chansons de geste du XIIe siècle," *Le Moyen Age* 30 (1975): 211–44; 407–45.

10. Is not "feudalism" based, as has been forcefully argued by P. Bonassie in *La Catalogne du milieu du Xe à la fin du XIIe siècle* (Toulouse, 1975), 2: 569–610, on the "subservience" of the peasants and on the exploitation of the workers? See also G. Duby, *Guerriers et paysans* (Paris, 1973) (English translation by Howard B. Clarke, *The Growth of the European Economy* [Ithaca, 1974]), especially pp.' 184–205, on this mode of production, which in a certain vocabulary is always called feudal, but which I feel should be called seigneurial, since it was predicated on the firmly established power to exploit the land and the men who cultivated it.

11. K. Schmid, "Zur Problematik von Familie, Sippe und Geschlecht, Haus und Dynastie beim mittelalterlichen Adel. Vorfragen zum Thema 'Adel und Herrschaft im Mittelalter'." *Zeitschrift für die Geschichte des Oberrheins* (1957).

12. G. Duby, "Lignage, noblesse et chevalerie au XIIe siècle dans la région mâconnaise. Une révision," *Annales, E.S.C.* 27 (July–October 1972): 803–23. Reprinted in G. Duby, *Hommes et structures au Moyen Age* (Paris, 1973), pp. 395–422. English translation in Robert Forster and Orest Ranum, eds., *Family and Society* (Baltimore, 1976), pp. 16–40.

13. G. Duby, "Remarques sur la littérature généalogique

en France au XIe et XIIe siècles," *Académie des Inscriptions et Belles Lettres, comptes rendus des séances de l'année 1967* (Paris, 1967). Reprinted in Duby, *Hommes et structures,* pp. 287–98.

14. Auguste-Joseph Bernard, ed., *Recueil des chartes de l'abbaye de Cluny,* 5 vols. (Paris, 1876–94), no. 3784.

15. Galbert of Bruges, *De multro, traditione et occisione gloriosi Karoli comitis Flandiarum,* ch. 13, in H. Pirenne, ed., *Histoire du meurtre de Charles le Bon, comte de Flandres (1127– 28)* (Paris, 1891), p. 23. English translation by James Bruce Ross, *The Murder of Charles the Good, Count of Flanders* (New York, 1957).

16. An example is Lambert of Wattrelos, when he evokes his ancestors. See G. Duby, "Structures de parenté et noblesse dans la France du Nord aux XIe et XIIe siècles, *Miscellanea Medievalia in memoriam J. F. Niermeyer* (Groningen, 1967). Reprinted in Duby, *Hommes et structures,* pp. 267– 85.

17. G. Duby, "Les 'jeunes' dans la société aristocratique. France du Nord-Ouest. XIIe siècle," *Annales, E.S.C.* 19 (September–October 1964): 835–46. Reprinted in Duby, *Hommes et structures,* pp. 213–25.

18. See, for example, the complementary nature of the rites of knighting and marriage, by which a "young man" was invested with power in his father's house: In about 1156 the crown prince Guigues, "jam adultus militari cingulo ab imperatore suscepto" and received "universis principibus et plebe," brought his new wife in a solemn procession into the house (*domus*) of his mother, the dowager, who at that time yielded authority to him. G. Boursequot-Giordanengo, "Une oeuvre narrative de la fin du XIIe siècle: la vie de la dauphine Clémence—Marie de Bourgogne," *Bulletin de la Société des Hautes Alpes* (Gap, 1975).

19. See the texts assembled, unfortunately without any concern for chronological order, by H. Oschinsky, *Der Ritter unterwegs und die Pflege der Gastfreundschaft im alten Frankreich* (Ph.D. diss., University of Halle, 1900). The daughters

or sisters of the knightly host "fondled" the hero at night after they had undressed him, sometimes pursuing him into his very bed. See, for instance, Gauvain and the Sister of the Little Knight:

> Tant on baisie et acole
> Que Gauvain la flour i quelli.
> (So much did they kiss and embrace
> That Gauvain robbed her of her flower.)
> [*Perceval*, 32191–2]

This is also confirmed by the biography of Saint Bernard by William of Saint-Thierry.

20. Andreas Capellanus, *De amore et amoris remedio*, bk. 2, ch. 12, Claude Buridant ed., *Traité de l'amour courtois* (Paris, 1974), p. 182. English translation by John Jay Parry, *The Art of Courtly Love* (New York, 1941).

21. G. Duby, Introduction to the *Roman de la Rose* (Paris, 1977).

22. On the differentiation of male and female attire, see H. Platelle, "Le problème du scandale: les nouvelles modes masculines aux XIe et XIIe siècles," *Revue Belge de Philologie et d'Histoire* 53 (1975): 1071–96. According to Andreas Capellanus, bk. 2, ch. 6 (Buridant ed., p. 160), it was normal for a knight to take a peasant woman, a servant girl, or a prostitute encountered by chance in a meadow. "This is tolerated in men because it is their habit and because their sex has the privilege of doing everything in this world that is dishonorable by nature." Such an attitude is condemned only if it is indulged too frequently or if the predator attacks a woman of higher social standing. But the shameless noble woman who gives herself to several men is to be rejected from the company of ladies.

23. In addition to the well-known studies by Adhémar Esmein, *Le mariage en droit canonique* (Paris, 1929–35); Jean Dauvillier, *Le mariage dans le droit classique de l'Eglise* (Paris, 1933); Pierre Daudet, *Etudes sur l'histoire de la juridiction*

matrimoniale: l'établissement de la compétence de l'église en matière de divorce et de consanguinité (Paris, 1941), see the most recent studies of this subject, to be published in the proceedings of the XXIV Settimana di studio, Spoleto, 1976.

24. This was true even in the very early Middle Ages, when Isidore of Seville was trying his best to find an explanation of this extension.

25. In some cases, the priest even gave the woman in marriage. See J. B. Molin and P. Mutembé, *Le rituel du mariage,* passim.

26. See the paper read by Pierre Toubert at the XXIV Settimana di studio, Spoleto, 1976.

27. Gerald of Cambrai, *Acta Synodi Atrebatensis,* ch. 10, "De connubiis," *PL* 142, 1299–1301.

28. Marriage constantly had to be defended against heretical propositions. Cf. Saint Bernard, in the sixty-fifth sermon on the Song of Songs, *PL* 183, 1095: To attack marriage is to open the doors to the debauchery of "concubinaries, perpetrators of incest, *seminiflues, masculorum concubitores,*" for chastity cannot be imposed on everyone.

29. Pierre Toubert, *Les structures du Latium médiéval* (Rome, 1973) 1: 741 ff.

30. According to P. Daudet and G. Picasso, speaking at the XXIV Settimana di studio, Spoleto, 1976.

31. Proof of this, for a later period and for a social stratum different from that under consideration here, is furnished by the register of punishments inflicted in the rural deanery of Droitwich in 1300 (R. Hilton, *A Medieval Society* [London, 1966] p. 265). Of the 107 persons, belonging to fifteen parishes, who were condemned to public whipping, 106 where punished for adultery or fornication.

Chapter II

1. Anselm of Canterbury, *Epistolae,* bk. 4, ep. 84 (1106–9), *PL* 159, 245. Cf. letter 83, written by Pascal II, concerning

the bad marriage of Robert, count of Meulan "sub prohibitione consanguinitatis uxorem duxerit, quam ejus propinquii prefato comiti remiserunt." The pope asked Anselm to release the two spouses from their sin.

2. Ivo of Chartres, *Epistola* 261 (ca. 1110), *PL* 162, 265–66.

3. *PL* 162, 495–96. Shortly thereafter, the same Hugh was excommunicated for violating the peace, and his father's land was placed under interdict, *ibid.*, 270.

4. The pact had been concluded, but the wedding had not yet taken place; "quos quidem parentes eorum gradu consanguinitatis esse testantur genitos, ut inter se nuptias contrahere non possint, nisi incestuosas et illicitas."

5. Cf. the interpolations added to this genealogy by Robert du Mont at the end of Book 8 of Guilleaume of Jumiège's *Histoire des ducs de Normandie* (Collection des mémoires relatifs à l'histoire de France . . . par M. Guizot, vol. 29 [Paris, 1826]). Du Mont wrote ca. 1149, at a time when the taste for genealogies was becoming firmly entrenched and when authors gave free rein to their imagination in elaborating them. See also Ordericus Vitalis, *Historiae ecclesiasticae libri tredecim,* bk. 3, chs. 3, 4, 5, Auguste Le Prévost, ed. (Paris, 1838–55).

6. This canon was adopted by Gratian, *Decretum* C. 35, q. 5, c. 2, in A. Friedberg, ed., *Corpus juris canonici* (Leipzig, 1871), 1: 1274. "Nam in septem gradibus, si canonice et usualiter numerentur, omnia propinquitatum, ultra quod nec consanguinitatis invenitur, nec omnia graduum reperiuntur (cf. the representations of the family tree in the manuscripts of Isidore of Seville), nec successio potest amplius prorogari, nec memorialiter ab aliquo generatio recordari. Quibus finibus, novae conjunctionis dicunt posse fieri initium, ι quasi fugientem possit revocare consanguinitatem." Gratian then advances the idea that canonical impediments encourage families to contract marriages outside the kin-group in order to widen the sway of that *caritas* which is natural within the family group.

7. The genealogies of dominant families that can be established—those, for example, that were published by M. Bur in *La formation du comté de Champagne (v. 950–v. 1150)* (Nancy, 1977)–show that in the eleventh and twelfth centuries kings, dukes, and counts were bound together by a network of close kinship relations.

8. Thus, Mathilde of Montgomery, sister of Hugh's grandmother, had married a half-brother (*frère uterin*) of William the Conqueror, her kinsman in the fourth degree.

9. Ivo of Chartres, *Epistola* 158, *PL* 162, 163–64.

10. It is the king, as head of the house, who will do the "counting" and "proving." "Et quia haec genealogia ab Avernensibus multoties est vobis computata obnixe precantur ut eadem computationem litteris apperte signatis per presentem portitorem episcopis ad curiam transmittatis. Nec enim decens est ut tantae nobilitatis sanguis tam publico incestu diutius polluatur et ad similem incestam perpetratum ferali exemplum carnalium voluntas animatur." Note that the letter dates from the time of Philip's conciliation with the Church and that it was written at the behest of both the king and Prince Louis.

11. Ivo of Chartres, *Epistola* 211, *PL* 162, 215–16.

12. Not in connection with these children, "who perhaps were not yet born at the time," but with their grandparents. "Computavit enim eam, ad suggestione domni papae, me audiente, quidam monachus Arvenensis (cf., *ep.* 158), nomine Castus, aetate maturus, de nobilibus terrae illius progenitus, vita et fama honestus."

13. "Since the king had renewed his intercourse with this woman, he was excommunicated at the Council of Poitiers by the cardinals John and Benedict."

14. Augustin Fliche, *Le règne de Philippe I, roi de France* (Paris, 1912).

15. This birth was due to the intercession of Saint Arnulf, the recluse of Soissons, who later became bishop. Once he had repudiated Bertha, Philip installed her at the château of

Montreuil, "quo illam dotaverat." At the same time, he granted his eleven-year-old son an appanage. According to Ordericus Vitalis, who wrote much later, Louis received Pontoise, Mantes, the entire Vexin, and even more, "totius regni curam, dum primo flore juventutis pubesceret, commisit." Here we have the legend of the king who, henceforth wallowing in debauchery, abdicated for all practical purposes at the time of his second marriage.

16. Bertrade's mother was also a descendant of Gonnor, and thereby of Richard of Normandy.

17. *Recueil des historiens de la France* [hereafter RHF] 15: 197. Philip agreed to "carnalis et illicitae copulae peccatum abjurare"; the separated spouses would henceforth meet only "sub testimonio personarum minime suspectarum."

18. Emile Mabille, ed., *Cartulaire de Marmoutiers pour le Dunois* (Châteaudun, 1874), n. 60.

19. Bibliothèque Nationale, Paris, MS. lat. 11792, fol. 143.

20. Ivo of Chartres, *Epistola* 13, *PL* 162, 26.

21. Ivo of Chartres, *Epistola* 15, ibid., 27–28.

22. Ivo of Chartres, *Epistola* 16, ibid., 28.

23. Ivo of Chartres, ibid.: "eam quam aliquis aliqua illicite pollutione maculavit, in conjugium ducere nulli licet vel licebit" (Gregory); "raptores raptas sibi jure vendicare non possunt" (Council of Châlon); "nuptias occultas factas non esse legitimas" (Hormisdas); "contubernia conjugia esse illarum mulierum, quae non sunt a parentibus traditae, et legibus dotatae, et a sacerdotibus solemniter benedictae" (Evaristus; these three rites are those that are prescribed by the rituals of marriage in the southern parts of Christendom); "qui mulierem rapuerit vel furatus fuerit aut seduxerit nunquam eam uxorem habeat" (Council of Aix).

24. Ibid.: "Virgines quae virginitatem non custodierint, si eosdem, qui eas violaverint, maritos acciperint, eo quod solas nuptias violaverint, post poenitentiam unius anni reconcilentur" (Eusebius); "posse sane fieri legitimas nup-

tias ex male conjunctis, honesto postea placito consequen-
te, manifestum est" (Augustine).

25. Ibid.: "quidam patres concubinas uxores fieri vetu-
erunt, honestatem conjugii commandantes et fedam concu-
binatus consuetudinem coercere cupientes, rigorem justi-
ciae teneri decreverunt."

26. Ivo of Chartres, *Epistola* 18, *PL* 162, 31–32. Roger was
just preparing to lift the anathema binding Simon of Melfa, a
subject of the diocese of Chartres, *adhuc in adulterio per-
durantem*. After the death of his first wife, Simon had married (*superinduxerat*) the woman who had earlier been his
mistress. Ivo has submitted the case to the pope and is
waiting for a reply. In the twenty-third letter, addressed to
Guy the Senechal, the intermediary who was attempting to
bring about a reconciliation between Philip and Ivo, the
bishop announces that "preparations have been completed
for the divorce between the king and his new wife."

27. P. Jaffé, ed., *Regesta pontificum romanorum ab condita
ecclesia ad annum post Christum natum MCXCVIII* (Leipzig,
1885–88) 2 vols., no. 5469.

28. Ivo of Chartres, *Epistola* 28, *PL* 162, 40–41.

29. Hugh of Flavigny in Burgundy, Clarius at Saint-
Pierre-le-Vif of Sens, Sigebert of Gembloux and Bernold of
Sankt Blasien in the Empire, the *Annals of Saint-Aubin* at
Angers.

30. Clarius, *Chronicon S. Petri Vivi*, in L. Duru, ed., *Bibliothèque historique de l'Yonne* (Auxerre, 1850–63), 2: 512;
Bernold, *Bernoldi Chronicon*, *MGH, SS* 5:461.

31. Clarius, *Chronicon S. Petri Vivi*.

32. Hugh of Flavigny, *Hugonis Chronicon*, lib. II, *MGH, SS*
8: 493.

33. Ibid.

34. Bertha died at Montreuil and was buried, the chronicles said, in a plebeian fashion (*more plebeio*).

35. Clarius, *Chronicon S. Petri Vivi*.

36. Bernold, *Chronicon*, *MGH, SS* 5:461.

37. Bernold, Ibid., p. 463, "propria uxore dimissa militis sui uxorem sibi in conjugium sociavit." Sigebert of Gembloux, *MGH. SS* 6: 367, is the only author to allude to adultery on the part of Bertrade: "vivente uxore sua superduxerat alteris viventis uxorem." Cf. Bernold, *MGH, SS* 5: 464: "abjurata adultera" in connection with Philip's spurious assertions of 1096 that he was dissolving the marriage.

38. *Recueil d'Annales angevines et vendômoises,* Louis Halphen, ed. (Paris, 1903), p. 42.

39. One of the authors in this tradition is Suger, *Vie de Louis VI le Gros,* Henri Waquet, ed. and trans. (Paris, 1964), bk. 12: If Philip did not ask to be buried at Saint-Denis, it was as an act of penance, because he felt that his conduct vis-à-vis the Church had not been what it should have been. Cf. the echo of this attitude (the king's speech) in Ordericus Vitalis, *Historiae ecclesiasticae libri tredecim,* bk. 11, ch. 34, Auguste le Prévost, ed. (Paris, 1838–55) 4: 283.

40. Pierre Béchin, a canon of Saint-Martin of Tours, claims that Philip stole (*abstulit*) Bertrade. André Salmon, ed., *Receuil des Chroniques de Touraine* (Tours, 1854), p. 55.

41. Paul-Alexandre Marchegay and André Salmon, eds., *Chroniques des comtes d'Anjou* (Paris, 1856–71), p. 142.

42. William of Malmsbury, *De gestis regum anglorum,* bk. 3, ch. 235, William Stubbs, ed. (London, 1889).

43. Ibid., ch. 257.

44. Ibid., ch. 235.

45. Ordericus Vitalis, *Historia ecclesiastica,* bk. 8, ch. 20, Le Prévost, ed., 3: 389.

46. William of Malmsbury, *De gestis regum anglorum,* bk. 3, chs. 235, 257, 345; Ordericus Vitalis, *Historia ecclesiastica,* bk. 5, Le Prévost, ed., 2: 404; bk. 8, ibid., 3: 387.

47. Ordericus Vitalis, *Historia ecclesiastica,* Le Prévost, ed., 3: 389, 390: "in flagitio graviter obduratus . . . . adulterioque putridus in malitia perduravit, ideoque dolori dentium et scatici multisque aliis infirmitatibus et ignominis merito subjacuit."

48. The *Gesta dominorum Ambascensium,* Marchegay and Salmon, eds., *Chroniques des comtes d'Anjou,* repeated and indeed embroidered the account of the *Gestes des comtes d'Anjou,* adding that Philip perpetrated a public adultery (*adulterium publicum exercuit*).

49. Philip undoubtedly failed to give up Bertha's domain, a fact that explains why the count of Flanders, Bertha's half-brother, "hated" him. (Cf. the testimony to that effect in *De Atrebatensi episcopatu restitutio, RHF* 14: 745). In 1106, Fulk of Anjou solemnly received Philip and Bertrade (*RHF* 12: 486). He himself had successively repudiated two of his first three wives.

50. *Vie de Louis le Gros par Suger,* bk. 1, Auguste Molinier, ed. (Paris, 1887).

51. It is difficult to believe that Bertrade's kinsmen did not agree to this marriage. It does appear, however, that since they had to reckon with Prince Louis, their behavior was rather guarded: While the first son of Philip and Bertrade received his father's name, the second was named neither Simon nor Amaury after his maternal grandfather or uncle; instead he was called Florus, a name that did not impose obligations on anyone.

52. In 1115 Bertrade gave to the monastery of Marmoutiers a forest which she "prius a rege Philippe in dote habuerat" (Martène, MS Paris, BN, lat. 12 879, fol. 24). In the document she calls herself "Bertrada regina, Philippi, regis Francorum uxor, et mater Fulconis junioris, Andegavorum comitis."

53. Ibid., "et postea ab ejus filio Ludovico rege illam redemerat."

54. Yet in 1004, at the same time when Constance, Bertha's daughter, was preparing to marry Bohémond of Antioch, Cecilia, Bertrade's daughter, was betrothed (*desponsata*) to Tancred. Her brother Philip—who was eleven years old at most—was engaged to the daughter of the seigneur of Montlhéry; to provide for his establishment, he was given the castle of Mantes, hitherto part of his elder

brother's appanage. As for the latter, Louis, the marriage to a daughter of the seigneur of Rochefort that was contemplated for him was by no means more prestigious than that of his brother.

55. This tradition was also a kind of revenge of Saint-Denis against the late king, Philip I, who had tended to favor Saint-Remy and Saint-Benoît-sur-Loir, where he had chosen to be buried.

56. Jaffé, ed., *Regesta pontificorum*, nos. 5636 and 5637.

57. Bernold, *Chronicon, MGH, SS* 5: 464.

58. Ivo of Chartres, *Epistolae* 141 and 144, *PL* 162, 148 and 150.

59. Ivo of Chartres, *Epistola* 245, *PL* 162, 153–54.

60. To strengthen his argument, Ivo cites the authorities: Augustine, Ambrose, Isidore of Seville, Nicholas II, Hincmar, John Chrysostomos, Novella 22, and Jerome's commentary on Hosea.

61. Ivo of Chartres, *Epistola* 155, *PL* 162, 158–59.

62. Cf. Ivo's letter 188, *PL* 162, 191–93: A woman who gives birth two or three months after marriage has no right to the "honor" of the *conjugium*; yet it is not possible to dissolve the union on these grounds.

63. Ivo of Chartres, *Epistola* 166, *PL* 162, 169–70. Mathilde, the daughter of Hugh the White, had been ceded (*tradita*) by her family to the chamberlain Galeran; Ponce, the nephew of the bishop of Troyes, had taken her despite her refusal and her tears; whereupon the bishop of Paris summoned his confrères, as well as Ponce and Mathilde. The young woman asserted that she had resisted and that her mother had supported her. Following the oaths of the oath-helpers, she was declared "libera a Pontii, non dicam conjugio sed contubernio." Ivo reports the facts (for one of Humbaud's parishioners wants to marry the young lady) "ne de preteritis nuptiis aliquod apud vos generetur scandalum."

64. Ivo of Chartres, *Epistola* 167, *PL* 162, 170. The man who had received the daughter of Pierre des Roches and had sworn to take her as his wife after a specified period of time

had married another woman. A marriage *cum filia familias de voluntate patris non dissentit* is indissoluble, unless forbidden on other grounds. The pact of *desponsatio* seals the union, as Ivo points out again in letters 161 and 246.

65. Marriage is based on mutual consent and on *dilectio*. But what if *dilectio* has disappeared? Ivo evokes such a case in connection with another problem. A man has unwittingly married a serf and has thereby fallen into serfdom. Naturally, he has come to hate his wife; is it possible to free him? Ivo replies that it is not possible (*Epistola* 221, *PL* 162, 226); but on another occasion (*Epistola* 253, *PL* 162, 258) agrees that since *dilectio* is impossible in such unions, they must be dissolved.

66. Ivo of Chartres, *Epistola* 167 to Hildebert of Lavardin, *PL* 162, 170.

67. Ivo of Chartres, *Epistola* 180, *PL* 162, 173. The Church was only concerned with adultery by men; was adultery on the part of women still exclusively subject to family law?

68. Ivo of Chartres, *Epistola* 125, *PL* 162, 137.

69. Ivo of Chartres, *Epistola* 230, *PL* 162, 233. "Domino nullum conjugatorum fieri posse divortium, excepta fornicationis causa. Sed, quia secundum apostolicam doctrinam, thorum immaculatum et honestum connubium opportet esse in omnibus, crescente religione christiana ad causas divortii additus est incestus."

70. Ivo of Chartres, *Epistola* 246, *PL* 162, 253–54.

71. Ibid., "Conjugium ex eo indissolubilis est, ex quo pactum conjugale firmatum est." Ivo cites Ambrose and Isidore.

72. Charles Pfister, *Etude sur le règne de Robert le Pieux* (Paris, 1885); Ferdinand Lot, *Etudes sur le règne de Hugues Capet et la fin du Xe siècle* (Paris, 1903); Ferdinand Lot, *Les derniers Carolingiens* (Paris, 1891).

73. Robert signed a charter together with Bertha in 1001. Between August 1003 and July 1004 Bertha called herself

"queen" in an act of donation to Marmoutiers; Pope John XVIII referred to her as *regina* in April 1004, according to Lot, *Hugues Capet,* p. 127, n. 2; but it is possible, of course, that she kept her title after the repudiation. Constance's eldest son was born in 1007.

74. Adelaide, sister of Geoffroy Grisejonelle and widow of Stephen of Gévaudan, had married Louis, son of King Lotharius, in 982, and the bishops had crowned her. When her husband abandoned her, she soon married the count of Arles without encountering any difficulties.

75. Odoranus of Sens, *Chronique,* in Robert Henri Bautier, ed., Odorannus, *Opera omnia* (Paris, 1973), pp. 100–102. Constance was at Thiel, a domain of Saint-Pierre-le-Vif of Sens, with her infant son Hugh: "Berta regina, dudum causa consanguinitatis a rege repudiata comperit, prosecuta est eum, sperans se, faventibus ad hoc quibusdum aulicis regis jussu apostolico restituram toto regio"; because of the intercession of Saint Savinian, the king returned from Rome and "propriam conjugem magis quam eatenus dilexit." Robert and Constance went together to Saint Jean d'Angély to venerate the recently discovered head of Saint John the Baptist.

76. *Richeri historiarum libri IIII,* 4, 87, *MGH, SS* 3: 651. At the age of twenty, Robert *facto divortio repudiavit* his first wife *eo quod anus esset;* he had to fight to take her dower (*dos*) away from her (ibid., 4, 88); "huius repudii scelus a nonnullis qui intelligentiae purioris fuere, satis laceratum eo tempore fuit, clam tamen, nec patenti refragatione culpatum." Richer's final notes (ibid., 657): Robert married Bertha "suorum consilio . . . . ea usus ratione quod melius sit parvum aggredi malum ut maxime evitetur; Berta Rotberto nubere volens Gerbertum consulit ac ab eo confutatur." As a zealous supporter of Gerbert, Richer wanted to make sure that none of the responsibility [for this marriage] was attributed to Gerbert.

77. A critical study of this enigmatic poem that was directed against Landri, the count of Nevers, can be found in Lot, *Hugues Capet,* p. 171, n. 1.

78. *Gregorii V Papae Litterae de Synodo Papiensi, MGH, SS* 3: 694. "Decretum est ut rex Rotbertus qui consanguineam suam contra interdictionem apostolicam in conjugium duxit add satisfactionem convocetur, cum episcopis his nuptiis incestis consentientibus. Si autem renuerint, communione privantur." Robert's and Bertha's grandmothers had been sisters.

79. Early in 998, Robert had yielded in the matter of the archbishopric of Reims (Abbo, *Epistola, PL* 139, 419–20). In the presence of Otto III, the Council of Rome threatened Robert and Bertha with anathema unless they separated; the *consecrator* of the marriage was the archbishop of Tours (*RHF* 10: 535).

80. After the Council of Pavia, the legate Leo had obtained from the king the reinstatement of Arnulf of Reims in exchange for the promise to confirm the king's *novum conjugium.* Gerbert, Letter 181, in Julien Havet, ed., *Lettres de Gerbert (983–997)* (Paris, 1889), p. 164.

81. Helgaud de Fleury, *Epitome,* in R. H. Bautier, ed., *Vie de Robert le Pieux* [Sources d'histoire médiévale I] (Paris, 1965), pp. 92–94.

82. Lot, *Hugues Capet,* pp. 170–71; O. Guillot, *Le comte d'Anjou et son entourage au XIe siècle* (Paris, 1972), 1: 21–29.

83. *Richeri historiarum libri IIII, MGH, SS* 3: 657, final notes: "Berta, Odonis uxor, suarum rerum defensorem et advocatum Rotbertum accepit"; in 1003 the king appointed Bertha's eldest son, Theobald, to the episcopal see of Chartres.

84. Guillot, *Le comte d'Anjou,* 1: 26.

85. In 1008, the abbot of Fleury and the bishop of Orleans were at odds over the matter of monastic autonomy; and Lieri, the archbishop of Sens, was criticized by the king for

his concept of the Eucharist. Queen Constance sided with the clerics and monks of Sens.

86. R. H. Bautier, "L'hérésie d'Orléans et le mouvement intellectuel au début du XIe siècle. Documents et hypothèses," *Actes du 95e congrès des Sociétés Savantes* (Paris, 1975); Guillot, *Le comte d'Anjou,* 1: 26. John of Ripoll claimed that the heretics "nuptiis detraebant"; Andrew of Fleury understood them to say: "nuptias cum benedictione non debere fieri, sed accipiat quiscumque qualiter voluerit." Abbot Gauzlin was led to make the statement: "nuptias non prohibeo, secunda matrimonia non dampno," Andrew of Fleury, *Vita Gauzlini,* ch. 56, in R. H. Bautier, ed. (Paris, 1969), p. 101.

87. Letter of Peter Damian to Desiderius of Monte Cassini, *RHF* 10: 493; Fragment of a History, ibid., p. 211.

88. *Historia gloriosissimi regis Ludovici VII,* ch. 25, Auguste Molinier, ed., in *Vie de Louis le Gros par Suger* (Paris, 1887), pp. 176–77. The baptism was celebrated the day after the birth, at Saint-Michel de la Place, by Maurice of Sully, with the abbots of Saint-Germain-des-Prés, Saint-Victor, and Sainte-Geneviève acting as godfathers and Constance, the king's sister, and two "widows of Paris" acting as godmothers.

89. Ibid., ch. 3 (Molinier, ed., p. 149).

90. Ibid., ch. 8 (Molinier, ed., p. 156); Cf. also Suger, *Vita Ludovici,* ch. 33, in Auguste Molinier, ed., *Vie de Louis le Gros par Suger* (Paris, 1887).

91. *Historia gloriosissimi regis Ludovici VII,* ch. 15, Molinier, ed., p. 163. . . . "accesserunt ad regem Ludovicum quidam propinqui et consanguinei sui et convenerunt eum, dicentes quod inter ipsum et Aleenoridem conjugem suam linea consanguinitatis erat, quod etiam juramento firmare promiserunt." Eleanor's great-grandfather had married the daughter of Robert, duke of Burgundy and brother of Henry I, Louis VII's great-grandfather. Louis and his wife thus were indeed cousins in the fourth and fifth degrees.

92. Present at the Council were the archbishops of Reims, Rouen, and Bordeaux, as well as some of their suffragans and a large number of the barons of the realm; the king's cousins swore to the kinship and the *copula matrimonii* was dissolved.

93. Eleanor had left Beaugency *celeriter,* sidestepped the advances of Theobald, count of Blois, at Blois, foiled the attempted ambush of Henry Plantagenet's brother Geoffrey who wanted to capture her, and finally reached Poitou, where she received Henry's marriage proposal. In July 1152, Louis and Geoffrey attacked Henry in Normandy.

94. Theobald of Blois consoled himself by marrying one of them; the other was given to the count of Troyes.

95. "Volens secundum divinam legem vivere (this a citation of Matthew 9:5) . . . propter spem succesive prolis que post ipsum regnum Francie regerat."

96. In 1156 "societata fuit in matrimonio Henrico, filio Henricis regis Anglorum et Aleenoridis . . . dispositione vero Romanae ecclesiae."

97. Ralph of Diceto says two weeks, *Ymagines historiarum,* W. Stubbs, ed., Rolls Series (London, 1876), 1: 303.

98. *Historia gloriosissimi regis Ludovici VII,* ch. 18 (Molinier, ed., p. 166).

99. The third wife was not the daughter of a king, but of Theobald of Champagne. Her brothers were the king's sons-in-law, but this affinity was not given any consideration whatsoever.

100. In 1154 at Orleans, the archbishop of Sens "in reginam inunxit [the new wife] et cum ipsa regem coronavit"; he performed the same ceremony at Paris in 1160, "missam etiam eodem die ibidem celebravit."

101. *Annales Cameracenses, RHF* 13: 507 :". . . pueriliter causidicans reginam . . . perpulchram, ab illo tempore quo Ierusalem perrexerant usque ad presens, convocans imprudenter hoc anno personas quasdam de regno, illisque

indiscrete cordis arcanum ebulliens, mox eorum usus consilio non sano, eam extemplo abjuravit."

102. *RHF* 12: 120: "Nihil turpe gessit, nisi quod Alienor uxorem suam repudiatam a thoro suo alienavit, alia in loco ejus post biennium subrogata." E. Vacandard, "Le divorce de Louis le jeune," *Revue des questions historiques* 47 (1890): 408–32, attempts to whitewash Saint Bernard. He imagines a mistake in the manuscript, postulating that a clause occuring a few lines earlier in a passage where Richard [the Poitevin] had mentioned the same three persons in connection with the second crusade, was repeated here. Geoffrey, the prior of Cîteaux and a cousin of Saint Bernard, had been elected to the episcopal see of Langres in 1138 by an electoral commission chosen by Innocent II with the greatest care, even though a monk of Cluny (about whom Saint Bernard says ugly things, *Epistola* 164, *PL* 182) had already been consecrated by the archbishop of Lyon and invested with the *regalia* by Louis VII. See E. Vacandard, "Saint Bernard et la royauté française," *Revue des questions historiques* 49 (1891): 353–409. These Cistercian maneuvers further embittered the relations between the pope and the White Monks on the one hand and the king of France and the Cluniacs on the other.

103. *RHF* 13, 43.

104. John of Salisbury, *Historia pontificalis, MGH, SS* 20: 534: ". . . familiaritas principis ad reginam et assidua fere sine intermissione colloquia regi suspicionem dederant, quae quidem ex eo magis invaluit, quod regina ibi voluit remanere."

105. Ibid.: "ipsa parentela mentionem faciens dixit illicitum esse ut diutius commanerent, quia inter eos cognatio in quarto gradu vertebatur et quinto."

106. Ibid.: "licet reginam affectu fere immoderato diligeret" (cf. p. 537: "reginam vehementer amabat et fere puerili modo").

107. Ibid.: "regno Francorum perpetuum opprobrium imminebat, si inter cetera infortunia rex disceretur spoliatus conjuge vel relictus."

108. Ibid.: "Hoc autem verbum antequam recederent auditum fuit in Francia, Bartholomeo bone memorie Laudunensi episcopo gradus cognationis computante, sed fida fuit an infidelis supputatio incertum est." (For this *computatio,* cf. below, the case of Ralph of Vermandois's divorce.)

109. Ibid., p. 537: "prohibens ne de cetero consanguinitatis inter eos mentio haberetur et confirmans matrimonium, tam verbo quam scripto sub anathematis interminatione inhibuit ne quis illud impugnans audiretur et ne quacumque solveretur occasione."

110. "Fecit eos in eodem lecto decumbere quam suo preciosissimis vestibus fecerat exornari."

111. Bernard of Clairvaux, *Epistola* 224, *PL* 182, 394.

112. In 1146 Bernard of Clairvaux had exhorted Louis VII not to marry his daughter to the son of the count of Anjou (who was Henry Plantagenet), "quia titulus consanguinitatis id prohibet, sicut veridica attestatione cognovimus, matrem reginae et puerum istum . . . in tertio consanguinitatis gradu inveniri." It is perfectly true that Henry's grandfather was the brother of Eleanor's grandmother, a fact that should have constituted an impediment to Eleanor's second marriage. But it was never mentioned by anyone in 1152.

113. *RHF* 15: 509–10.

114. *RHF* 13: 293. Louis objected to Eleanor's remarriage because "habebat enim duas filias de ea, et ideo nolebat ut ab aliquo illa filio exciperet, unde predicte filie exhederentur."

115. *Historia Hierosolymitana* (written in 1169–81), bk. 16, ch. 27, in *PL* 201, 670. Raymond of Antioch "aut violenter aut occultis machinationibus ab eo rapere voluerit" Eleanor, "quae una erat de fatuis mulieribus . . . mulier imprudens et contra dignitatem regiam legem negligens maritalem, tori conjugalis oblita."

116. William of Newburgh, *De rebus Anglicis Libri II, RHF* 13: 101–2. ". . . juvenis animum suae formae venustate prestrictum . . . ." This love cooled down upon the king's return from the east, "non sine infecti negotii dedecore; illa maxime ex moribus regis offensa, et causante se monacho non regi nupsisse." Dreaming of new nuptials "suis magis moribus congruas" with the duke of Normandy, Eleanor took the initiative. "Habens potestatem cui vellet nubendi," she left her two daughters to their father and married Henry in all haste, fearing that a *solemnis preparatio nuptiarum* would bring to light some impediment.

117. Gervais began to write his chronicle in 1188 (*RHF* 13: 125). The *discordia* worsened during the voyage overseas "ex quibusdam forte quae melius tacenda sunt . . . . Divortio . . . labore multo et artificioso juramento in facie ecclesie solemniter celebrato," Eleanor let Henry know that she was free, "missis clanculo ad ducem nunciis . . . . Dicebatur enim artificiosam repudiationem illam ex ipsius procecisse ingenio. Dux vero generositate femine et maxime dignitatum que eam contigebant, cupiditate illectus . . ."

118. Gerald of Wales, *De instructione principis*, bks. 2 and 3, in *RHF* 18: 155–56: "qualiter, quaeso, ex copula tali felix potuit prosapia nasci."

119. Henry was responsible: "indebite subtraxit [Louis VII's wife] sibique de facto conjugali vinculo copulaverit" (ibid., p. 128); but the sin was caused by Eleanor, whose conduct toward both her successive husbands was bad (ibid.). "Comes Andegavensis, quando senescallus Francie fuit, abusus fuerat Alienor"; he is said to have forbidden Henry to touch her "tum quia domini sui sponsa, tum etiam quoniam a patre suo fuit ante cognita. Ad cumulum igitur excessum nimis enormium sic dictam Francie reginam rex Henricus adulterino concubitu, sicut fama dispersit, polluere presumpsit, dominoque suo sic ipsam retraxit, sibique maritaliter eadem de facto copulavit." Note that Gerald depicts Henry's conduct as that of a *juvenis* in the courtly game of love (cf. below, ch. 3).

120. *Continuatio Aquicinensis, MGH, SS* 6: 406.

121. Helinand of Froidmont, *Chronicon, PL* 212, 1057–58.

122. It was probably at this time that an ecclesiastical ritual of marriage took shape in northern France. Possibly based on English models, this ritual and its diffusion seem to have been promoted with particular vigor by the dioceses of Cambrai-Arras and Laon, as well as those of Normandy. Actually, however, the evidence for such a movement is very indistinct. It comes from manuscripts that are difficult to date, since they are among the rare remains of dilapidated episcopal libraries, and it is extremely difficult to ascertain when and where they were in use. Cf. Molin and Mutembé, *Le rituel du mariage.*

123. Cf. Gabriel Le Bras, "Mariage," in *Dictionnaire de Théologie Catholique* (Paris, 1908–50).

124. Hugh of Saint-Victor, *De beate Marie virginitate, PL* 176, 859–64.

125. Hildebert of Lavardin, *De communi consensu,* sermon preached at the occasion of the Council of Chartres in 1124, *PL* 170, 293–94.

126. Herimann of Saint-Martin of Tournai, *Liber de restauratione monasterii sancti Martini Tornacensis, MGH, SS* 14: 343.

127. "Fama hujus parjurii per totam disseminata regionem, etiam ad apostolicam audientiam dilata est per comitem Theobaldum Burgundionum principem. Hujus enim erat neptis ea quam Radulphus comes dimiserat et dedecus repulse eum spectabat."

128. Cf. Elphège Vacandard, *Vie de Saint Bernard, abbé de Clairvaux* (4th ed; Paris, 1927).

129. Bernard of Clairvaux, *Epistola* 216, *PL* 182, 380.

130. Bernard of Clairvaux, *Epistola* 217, *PL* 182, 381. Theobald, his back to the wall after Louis VII's successful offensive, was made to "sub jurejurande promittere" that he would have the excommunication lifted. Very wise men

advised him, telling him that it would be very easy "et absque laesione ecclesiae" to arrange matters, "dum in manu [papae] sit, eandem denuo sententiam, quae juste data fuit, incontinenti statuere et irretractabiliter confirmari: quatenus et ars arte deludatur."

131. Bernard of Clairvaux, *Epistola* 220 to Louis VII, *PL* 182, 385. The king had asked him to prevent this renewal of the anathema. "Non ideo tamen debemus facere mala ut veniant bona." Why did the king accuse Theobald? Theobald had indeed obtained Ralph's absolution, unjustified though it was; nor had he asked for the second excommunication.

132. Bernard of Clairvaux, *Epistola* 221, to the bishop of Soissons, *PL* 182, 388.

133. Cf. Herimann of Tournai, *Liber de restauratione,* on the Flemish marriage: "licet rex Francorum conjugium niteretur dissolvere, tertio gradu consanguinitatis dicens eos invicem propinquos esse."

134. Bernard of Clairvaux, *Epistola* 224, *PL* 182, 393. It is here that Bernard accuses Louis VII of living with his cousin in the third degree.

135. Ibid.: "Si consanguinitatis sit, nescio; scienter enim illicita matrimonia nec laudavi umquam nec laudo; sed sciatis vos . . . prohibere horum nuptias . . . exarmare ecclesiam est, et multam illi subtrahere fortitudinem."

136. Bernard of Clairvaux, *Epistola* 371, *PL* 182, 575–76.

137. *Historia pontificalis, MGH, SS* 20: 521: ". . . auxilio et consilio diaconorum cardinalium Johannis Paparonis, Gregorii de Sancto Angelo, optinuit, non sine suspitione intervenientis pecunie."

138. Ibid.: The pope "benevolentiam mulieris et partis sue captare visus est, dicens se id agere ut illa debitam consolationem recipiat."

139. Ibid.: ". . . Parentelam, quam alia vice vitaverant, tactis evangeliis juraturi."

140. John W. Baldwin, *Masters, Princes, and Merchants: The Social Views of Peter the Chanter and His Circle* (Princeton, 1970), especially vol. 1, pp. 332–34.

141. R. Davidsohn, *Philip II August von Frankreich und Ingeborg* (Stuttgart, 1888).

142. K. F. Werner, "Die Legitimität der Karolinger und die Entstehung des *Reditus ad stirpem Karoli,*" *Die Welt als Geschichte* 12 (1952).

143. Rigord, *Gesta Philippi Augusti,* in A. François Delaborde, ed., *Les oeuvres de Rigord et de Guilleaume de Breton, historiens de Philippe-Auguste,* 2 vols. (Paris 1882–85), 1: 124: "quibusdam, ut dicitur, maleficiis per sorcerias impeditus."

144. Ibid., p. 133.

145. These genealogies are published in Davidsohn, *Philip II Augustus,* pp. 297–312. Professor Bernard Guenée of the Sorbonne is presently engaged in a new study of them.

146. G. Duby, *Le Dimanche de Bouvines* (Paris, 1973), p. 149 ff.

147. R. Tenbrock, *Eherecht und Ehepolitik bei Innozenz III* (Münster/Westfalen, 1933). Baldwin, *Masters, Princes, and Merchants,* 1: 332–37.

Chapter III

1. Pierre Toubert, *Les structures du Latium Médiéval,* (Rome, 1973), 1: 749–68; D. Owen-Hughes, "Urban Growth and Family Structures in Medieval Genoa," *Past and Present* 66 (1975): 3–28.

2. I have used this work several times: G. Duby, "Les 'jeunes' " (cited in ch. 1, n. 17); "Structures de parenté et noblesse" (cited in ch. 1, n. 16).

3. F. L. Ganshof, "A propos de la chronique de Lambert d'Ardres," *Mélanges . . . F. Lot* (Paris, 1925), has demolished the argument of W. Erben, who, in "Zur Zeitbestimmung Lamberts von Ardres," *Neues Archiv* 44, wanted to date this text from the fourteenth century.

4. G. Duby, "Littérature généalogique" (cited in ch. 1, n. 13).

5. Lambert of Ardres, *Historia comitum Ghisnensium, MGH, SS* 24, 563: "Ad laudem . . . et gloriam et honorem Ghisnensium et Ardentium procerum." This work is clearly a monument to the glory of a small state that proclaimed its autonomy, situated as it was between the county of Flanders and the county of Boulogne during the political upheavals on the eve of Bouvines. It was appropriate for such a celebration to be composed in Latin.

6. Cf. Urban T. Holmes, "The Arthurian Tradition in Lambert d'Ardres," *Speculum* 25 (1950): 100–104.

7. In the form: "X. duxit in uxorem Y., que concepit et peperit Z^1, Z^2, Z^3."

8. *Historia comitum Ghisnensium*, ch. 127, p. 624.

9. Ibid., ch. 91.

10. Ibid., ch. 67, p. 593.

11. Ibid., ch. 149, p. 638.

12. The *benedictio lectuli nuptialis* is among the oldest attestations of priestly intervention in the marriage ceremony. Cf. Molin and Mutembé, *Le rituel du mariage,* p. 256 (cited in ch. 1, n. 4).

13. *Historia comitum Ghisnensium,* ch. 123, p. 622: "in ludicris et jocis cum jocunditate et exaltatione solemnes celebraverunt nuptias."

14. One of these was Saint-Léonard of Guines, founded in 1117 by the countess. Out of the convent of Bourbourg came the heiress of that estate when she was married; she had spent her youth there, "non tamen nutrienda quam moribus erudienda et liberalibus studiis imbuenda." Ibid., ch. 122, p. 621.

15. Ibid., ch. 89, p. 603.

16. Ibid., n. 1.

17. The beauty of the girl whom he has ravished is an excuse for the abductor, whose sin the Church will punish less severely. Cf. Alain de Lille, *Liber poenitentialis,* bk. 1, ch. 27, or J. Longère, ed., *Analecta medievalia Namurcensia* 18

(Louvain, 1965), 2: 34: "Utrum illa in qua peccavit sit pulchra vel non?".

18. *Historia comitum Ghisensium,* Ibid. ch. 134, p. 629.

19. Ibid., ch. 113, p. 615: "contubernium debitum."

20. Ibid., ch. 139. Cf. also Arnulf II of Ardres, "filiis suis, tam in venere delectationis conceptis quam in nobili uxore Gertrude procreatis, militibus factis," ibid., ch. 126, p. 623.

21. Ibid., ch. 84, p. 601.

22. Ibid., ch. 64, p. 593: "Pre omnibus et in omnibus in gloriosa liberorum jucundabatur propagine, et in eorum promotione ferventiori nimirum stimulo et sollicitudine animum irritabat atque urgebat."

23. Ibid., ch. 43, pp. 582–83.

24. Ibid., ch. 149, p. 637: Arnulf married Beatrice of Bourbourg "ad consilium patris sui," but also with the consent of the four Béthune brothers (among them the poet Conon). The latter were the brothers of Beatrice's mother, the dowager widow of the last châtelain of Bourbourg, whose heiress Beatrice was. Moreover, the son of Beatrice's father's older sister also gave his consent, as the eldest male of the bloodline of the châtelains of Bourbourg.

25. The vassalic connection was felt to be of the same nature as family ties. The *senior* first married off his own children, then also the young men "provided for" in his house. Another consideration was service to the fief, that is, the functioning of a system of obligations that was fully developed in this region during the second half of the twelfth century.

26. Henry I had already laid claim to this right; but the custom "in gallicana et anglicana regione" was denounced as a recent development by the Parisian masters of the late twelfth century. Cf. Baldwin, *Masters, Princes, and Merchants,* 1: 248–49; 2: 178, n. 133.

27. *Historia comitum Ghisnensium,* ch. 86, p. 601.

28. Ibid., chs. 97, 98, 99, 103.

29. Ibid., ch. 48, p. 585: " O gloriosissimi patris affectum! O per omnia praedicandam filie subjectionem."

30. Ibid., ch. 66, p. 584: "filias ad magne generationis sobolem procreandam progenitas."

31. Ibid., chs. 133, 72, 79.

32. Ibid., ch. 122.

33. Ibid.

34. Ibid., ch. 67, p. 594.

35. Henry of Bourbourg, for instance, in order to marry his daughter to the seigneur of Ardres, whose alliance he sought, separated this daughter from an English lord to whom she was married. A delegation of priests and knights was sent to the Englishman, "et exposita ei vie causa egritudinem uxoris sue cum aliis sufficientibus causis ei pretulerunt. Accepto die et statuto judicario ordino et ecclesiastico, separati sunt." (Ibid., ch. 60, p. 591.)

36. Ibid., chs. 72, 79.

37. Ibid., ch. 15.

38. Ibid., ch. 123, p. 622.

39. Ibid., ch. 10; ch. 11, p. 568.

40. Ibid., ch. 93, pp. 604, 605.

41. Ibid., chs. 96, 94: "inconstantia et fallacia muliebris perfidia"; "perfida."

42. The Church was much more punctilious concerning chastity within marriage, a sacred thing. Cf. Andreas Capellanus, *De amore et amoris remedio,* bk. 1, ch. 6 (Buridant ed., p. 109): The answer to the question: is love not better within marriage than in courtly love? is No; for if the spouses take pleasure, they "sin." Better yet: "Those who sully a sacred thing by abusing it are punished more severely than those who habitually commit excesses. And the fault is more grievous in a married woman than in others. It is true, as the Church teaches, that a man who loves his wife too passionately is guilty of adultery." Cf. Peter Lombard, *Sententiae,* bk. 4, 31, 6, *PL* 192, 920: ". . . in matrimonio spera liberorum concessa sunt, voluptas autem quae de meretricum amplexibus capiantur in uxore sunt damnatae." Cf. also Alain de Lille, *Summa de arte predicatoria, PL* 210, 193: "vehemens amator uxoris adulter est."

43. This ambiguity is evident in the secular literature produced at that time. Between 1160 and 1220, two currents existed side by side in northern France: the older tradition of opposition to marriage and the more recent tendency that made courtly love a part of the conjugal bond. In *Perceval,* "courtly love is no longer seen as a force that ennobles and educates the knight but on the contrary as a power that threatens his very existence," T. Ehlert and G. Meissburger, "Perceval et Parzival," *Cahiers de Civilisation médiévale* 18 (1975): 197–227.

44. Hugh of Saint-Victor, *De amore sponsi ad sponsam, PL* 176, 987.

Sources of Illustrations

Frontispiece: "Marriage Scene." Detail from an illuminated manuscript. Ms. 372, f. 168. Laon, Bibliothèque communale.

Page 1: "Betrothal Scene." Detail from an illuminated manuscript. Ms. C. 967, f. 173v. Cambrai, Bibliothèque municipale.

Page 24: "Seduction Scene." Detail from an illuminated manuscript. Ms. 10.133, f. 310. Baltimore, Walters Art Gallery.

Page 82: "Marriage Scene." Detail from an illuminated manuscript. Ms. lat. 2491, f. 478. Vatican, Biblioteca Apostolica Vaticana.

These illustrations are reprinted with permission and appear in Anthony Melnikas, *The Corpus of the Miniatures in the Manuscripts of Decretum Gratiani*, Volume 3 (Rome: 1975).

Library of Congress Cataloging in Publication Data

Duby, Georges.
  Medieval marriage.

  (The Johns Hopkins symposia in comparative
history; 11)
  Originally presented in French as lectures at
Johns Hopkins University, Apr. 12, 13, and 15, 1977.
    1. Marriage—France—History. 2. France—
Social life and customs. 3. France—History—
Medieval period, 987–1515. I. Title. II. Series.
HQ513.D8   301.42'0944   77–17255
ISBN 0–8018–2049–9
ISBN 0–8018–4319–7 (pbk.)